Georgia Law requires Library materials
to be returned or replacement costs paid.
Failure to comply with this law
is a misdemeanor. (O.C.G.A. 20-5-53)

Skinheads

Recent Titles in
Guides to Subcultures and Countercultures

Guides to
Subcultures and
Countercultures

Skinheads

A Guide to an American Subculture

Tiffini A. Travis and Perry Hardy

GREENWOOD

AN IMPRINT OF ABC-CLIO, LLC
Santa Barbara, California • Denver, Colorado • Oxford, England

Library of Congress Cataloging-in-Publication Data

Travis, Tiffini A., 1971–
    Skinheads : a guide to an American subculture / Tiffini A. Travis and Perry Hardy.
        p. cm. — (Guides to subcultures and countercultures)
    Includes bibliographical references and index.
    ISBN 978–0–313–35953–8 (cloth : alk. paper) — ISBN 978–0–313–35954–5 (ebook)
1. Skinheads—United States. 2. Punk culture—United States. 3. White supremacy movements—United States. 4. Subculture—United States. I. Hardy, Perry. II. Title.
HV6439. U5T74   2012
306′.1—dc23   2011050445

ISBN: 978–0–313–35953–8
EISBN: 978–0–313–35954–5

16 15 14 13 12   2 3 4 5

This book is also available on the World Wide Web as an eBook.
Visit www.abc-clio.com for details.

Greenwood
An Imprint of ABC-CLIO, LLC

ABC-CLIO, LLC
130 Cremona Drive, P.O. Box 1911
Santa Barbara, California 93116-1911

This book is printed on acid-free paper ∞

Manufactured in the United States of America

Contents

Series Foreword

From beatniks to flappers, Zoot Suiters to punks, this series brings to life some of the most compelling countercultures in U.S. history. Designed to offer a quick, in-depth examination and current perspective on each group, the series aims to stimulate the reader's understanding of the richness of the American experience. Each book explores a countercultural group that plays a critical role in American life and introduces the reader to its historical setting and precedents, the ways in which it was subversive or countercultural, and its significance and legacy in American history.

Webster's Ninth New Collegiate Dictionary defines counterculture as "a culture with values and mores that run counter to those of established society." Although some of the groups covered in this series might be described as primarily subcultural, they were selected for inclusion here because they have not existed in a vacuum. Rather, they have advocated for rules that methodically opposed mainstream culture, or lived by those ideals to the degree that it became impossible for them not to influence the society around them. In short, these groups have left their marks—both positive and negative—on the fabric of American culture. Volumes in this series cover such groups as hippies and beatniks, who influenced popular culture, literature, and art; the eco-socialists and radical feminists, who worked toward social and political change; and even groups such as the Ku Klux Klan, who left mostly scars on the American psyche and landscape.

A lively alternative to narrow historiography and scholarly monographs, each volume in the *Subcultures and Countercultures* series can be described as a "library in a book," containing both essays and browsable reference materials, including primary documents, to enhance the research process and bring the content alive in a variety of ways. Written for students and general readers, each volume includes engaging illustrations, a timeline of critical events in the subculture, topical essays that illuminate aspects of the subculture, a glossary of subculture terms and slang, biographical sketches of the key players involved, and primary source excerpts—including speeches, writings, articles, first-person accounts, memoirs, diaries, government reports, and court decisions—that offer a contemporary perspective on each group. In addition, each volume includes an extensive bibliography of current recommended print and nonprint sources appropriate for further research.

Preface

The purpose of this book is to give a firsthand, authoritative account of how the skinhead cult emerged in the United States. Each chapter examines a particular aspect of the subculture from a historical perspective and provides insight from actual skinheads who were there. The scope of the discussion covers the development of the skinhead subculture in England and its subsequent adoption by large numbers of youths across the United States. The book contains topical chapters that explore various facets of the subculture, including why youths choose to label themselves skinheads; how this subculture has influenced popular culture, including music, film, and fashion; and how racism altered the status of the skinhead movement, changing the public's perception of it from a subculture to a pariah. The final chapter, on the future of skinheads, examines the current state of the subculture and suggests where the authors believe it is headed. The last sections of the book provide snapshots of various aspects of the scene, including the first skinhead gangs, notable bands, and unique factions in the skinhead subculture. To enable further and more in-depth research of skinheads, the annotated bibliography lists additional sources of information, including books, scholarly and popular articles, and websites. The primary documents section includes sources that provide firsthand accounts from skinheads in the 1980s and 1990s. Through the wealth of information in this book, we hope to supply the reader with a complete image of what it was like to be a skinhead from the inception of this subculture to the present day.

Acknowledgments

We would like to thank our families for their patience and understanding throughout this whole process. Tiffini Travis: Jaelin, Raphael and Martina Travis Blount, Rozanna and Tracina Travis, Ronald and Rosalia Travis. Perry Hardy: Kelly and daughter Willa.

We would also like to acknowledge the current and past skinheads who helped with the creation of this reference title. Without their firsthand experience and collective knowledge, it would have been difficult to write this book: Phil, Carl, Chris Templar, Bohdan Zachryj, Skip Behanna, Eddie Oaks, Chris and Ashley Nutter, Frank2Far, Frank of Crash and Burn, Ray Guins, Sab Grey, Sean (Orlando), Roger Miret, Mike Ledger, Chuck and Laura McCann, Chris Piccolini, Vinnie Stigma, Jimmy G (Murphy's Law), Danny Diablo, Mike Erikson, Frank and Paol from Oxblood, Lars Frederiksen, Anthony "Cheeks" Buttaci, Pressure Point, Eric "Gonzo" Gonzales, Danny (Toughskins), Shawn Stern, Cliff Shirk, Jim Heywood, Chris Schaefer, Tomiko, Doug Kane, John Joseph (Cro-Mags), Gonzo Rodriguez, Sid Collins, Gardner Lund, Joel Loya, Marty J., Marty Williams, Adrian A., Jimmy Shelton, Darren Reggae, Symond Lawes, Alan Guest, Michael Finnie, Mike and Denny Crowell, Dwayne (Chicago), Eddie H., Mike Chamberlain, Heather Fails, Matt C., Andy Anthrax, Nos and Mike Silva from Hawaii, Tim K., Rick and Sabi Hendricks, Stan Corona, Boxer H. Greg Lee, Hollin Lange, Martin R., Greg Narvas, Grover (Cincinnati), Ted (San Francisco), Shane (Chicago), John Johnson, LA Bootboys, Swingin Utters, Toughskins, Stormy, Kevin Mills, Dave Hawk, Sean Wheeler, Jake Fuller, Wil C., Eric Z., Grandpa Skin (San Diego), Eddie (WWAC), Tonya (RIP), Lajuan Harris, Mike Crenshaw, Pan (Portland), Donny (Orange County), Sean (San Diego), Heather (San Diego), Scotti Lyons, Brooke Bardin, Erik O'Neal, Justin Cook, Bo Bauer, Dannyboy Smith, Scott Davis (Broken Heroes), Kevin McNeice, Randy Blazak, and Eric Andersen. Some names have been omitted at the request of the individuals—you know who you are and we thank you, too!

Lastly, we would like to thank the current and past members of some of the early crews and skinhead gangs who shared their experience with us: Bomber Boys, Minneapolis Baldies, RASH, American Firm, CASH, SHARP, THA, American Front, Warskins, ARA (Dallas), ARA (Chicago) Confederate Hammerskins, Hammerskin Nation, Doc Marten Skinheads, Carson Skins, Pitbulls (Chicago), Northside Firm (CA), Unity (SGV), Fear City, Santa Cruz Centurions, NISH, Rose City, and SHOC.

Introduction

The skinhead subculture was born in England in the late 1960s as an offshoot of the mod culture. Skinheads were distinct from other British subcultures due to their uniform of boots, jeans, braces (suspenders), and the trademark shaved head. Their style was an exaggerated version of the traditional unskilled laborer. One of the first scholars to research skinheads, sociologist Mike Brake, classified skinheads as a "traditional working class delinquent subculture" and documented five traits that defined first-generation British skinheads: (1) toughness and violence; (2) football (soccer); (3) ethnocentrism; (4) Puritan work ethic; and (5) a cynical worldview.[1] According to author Nick Knight, skinheads first appeared as a distinct youth subculture in 1968. He states in his book *Skinhead*, "In establishing their own style, the younger brothers of mods adopted certain elements of mod style, combined them with items from traditional working clothes, borrowed some influences from the West Indian blacks and became skinheads."[2]

Skinheads emerged in America during the punk movement of the early 1980s. Some of the first skinheads documented in the United States included Harley Flanagan from New York and Sab Grey from Washington, D.C. Both interacted with skinheads from England during the late 1970s and were exposed to the subculture from its

British skinheads, Piccadilly Square, 1980 (Gavin Watson).

country of origin. The subculture that eventually became American skinheads was a blend of the British subculture with American values and norms. Since their emergence in the United States, skinheads have become one of the most vilified and maligned American subcultures ever documented. Largely due to media publicity and external groups capitalizing on their notoriety, skinheads have become widely associated with hate crimes and acts of violence. In reality, the skinhead subculture is more complex than an army of pubescent youths with shaved heads and boots. This group's emergence from the punk movement to its own distinct subculture is significant in that skinheads are the embodiment of "Reagan-era" America built on a fear of communism, fierce nationalism, and the declining working class. The youths who make up the American version of the subculture vary greatly from their counterparts in post-war Britain.

British Skinheads

In England, there were two waves of the skinhead cult. From its inception, the skinhead subculture was largely based around music. The first group appeared in the late 1960s as an offshoot of the mod subculture, and largely died out by 1972.

The second wave arrived in the late 1970s and early 1980s. These skinheads differed from the first generation, in that they were not influenced as much by mod as they were by the growing punk and 2Tone Ska scenes in London. Punk lent itself to violence through its embrace of aggressive music and teenage angst. Skinheads reflected this new influence by combining the exaggerated imagery of the original skinhead style with punk. They took the boots and braces and jeans of the late 1960s and added closer-cropped hair, bomber jackets, and tattoos. The popularity of the 2Tone movement helped spread the look of skinheads to all parts of the United Kingdom. Symond Lawes, a British skinhead notes, "I became a skinhead and there was only one other skinhead in my estate in 1978. By the following year every kid in England was a skinhead."

At the same time the subculture was growing, England was experiencing an influx of immigrants from India; the backlash to this wave of newcomers from the native British population was reflected in the skinhead subculture. Zeig Heiling and "Paki bashing" were sensationalized by the media. The growth of the right-wing National Front and its recruitment of youth merely increased the amount of

First-generation skinheads, Palm Springs, California, 1983 (Sean Wheeler).

conflict present in the skinhead subculture. Punk shows and Ska shows were marred by skinhead violence. Even American newspapers covered the race riots that exploded in London in 1981, including the Southhall riot, which was sparked after a canceled Oi! music concert featuring notable skinhead bands, the 4skins, the Last Resort and the Business.

While there is little doubt that North Americans, especially Canadians as part of the British Commonwealth, were exposed to skinhead subculture in the late 1960s and during the initial resurgence of this movement in 1978, it did not take hold as a youth cult in the United States until the arrival of punk. Groups of youths in the early years of the American hardcore punk scene had shaved heads, but cannot be categorized as skinheads because they did not consciously adopt the lifestyle or dress that defines the subculture. Eventually, American youths began to emulate the skinhead style that was seen in the United Kingdom.

Origins of American Skinheads

As with their British counterparts, the roots of American skinheads can be found in the hardcore punk and Ska movements. While skinheads in the United States were heavily influenced by their British counterparts, the impact of American hardcore music mutated the original British skinhead style into something quite distinct from the U.K. version. In the early years of the American scene, two types of skinhead emerged. The first subgroup was influenced by hardcore music, and the other was influenced by 2Tone Ska. Both breeds of skinheads appeared simultaneously in various localities as early as 1981.

The second generation of skinheads in the United States appeared after 1986. By this time, youths had an established skinhead subculture to emulate. While the first generation of skinheads in the United States was influenced primarily by English skinheads, the second generation of American skinheads owes its popularity almost entirely to the early New York hardcore scene.

The racist element of British skinheads from the 1980s, while always present in the United States, did not fully articulate itself until

1985. Due to the growing divisions within the scene caused by the overtly racist rhetoric, new skinheads were more likely to consciously align themselves with one side or the other. By 1988, both strains of skinheads could be found in almost every major U.S. city. Initially there was an uneasy "unity" between both groups; however, by 1988 the factions within the skinhead scene broke into open warfare.

The increased awareness of skinheads in the United States resulted in law enforcement and groups such as the Anti-Defamation League (ADL) tracking the rise of racist skinheads. They estimated the number of racist skinheads in the United States to be between 3,300 and 3,500 in 1987; by 1997, however, growth of skinhead groups had stagnated, with membership holding at between 2,500 and 3,500. These sources also noted that "non-racist skinheads considerably outnumber the racist ones in most areas of the country."[3] The process for tracking skinhead populations included self-identification or data from law enforcement agencies. Due to this method of data collection, these numbers can be seen only as general estimates of the true number of youths claiming to be skinheads in the United States.

Regardless of the actual number of skinheads, the expansion of the subculture is evident by examining its growth regionally since 1980. The second wave of skinheads is still active in most major cities in the United States, Europe, and North America and as far away as Malaysia and Peru.

Notes

1. Mike Brake, "The Skinheads: An English Working Class Subculture," *Youth & Society* 6 (1974), 190.
2. Nick Knight, *Skinhead* (London: Omnibus, 1982), 8.
3. Irwin Suall, et al., *Shaved for Battle: Skinheads Target America's Youth*. ADL special report (New York: Anti-Defamation League of B'nai B'rith/Civil Rights Division, 1987), x.

Timeline

1969 The original British skinheads emerge from the mod and rudeboy subcultures.

The New York Times reports on the new youth subculture called skinheads.

1970 *The New York Times* and *Time* magazine both have features on skinheads in England.

1978 The second generation of British skinheads emerges.

1980 Harley Flanagan becomes a skinhead during a tour of Ireland with his band the Stimulators, and brings the style home to New York City. New York has perhaps the first documented skinhead presence in the United States. Skinheads also begin appearing in Los Angeles and Washington, D.C.

Iron Cross forms in Washington, D.C., becoming the first skinhead Oi! band in the United States.

The 2Tone band the Specials performs on Saturday Night Live

Rock journalist Garry Bushell coined the term "Oi!" to describe a new type of punk music

1981   Skinheads appear in a number of other cities, such as Detroit, Chicago, San Francisco, and Boston. Bands greatly influenced by the British skinhead scene—such as the Effigies from Chicago, Youth Brigade from Los Angeles, and Negative Approach from Detroit—form

1982   The film *Dance Craze*, which features 2Tone bands, is released in the United States.

Iron Cross releases its debut EP *Skinhead Glory*, becoming the first American skinhead band to release a record.

Four skinheads from New York form a band called Agnostic Front, which will become perhaps the most popular and influential American skinhead band ever.

Warzone is formed on the Lower East Side of New York City by Agnostic Front drummer Ray "Raybeez" Barbieri. It will rise to prominence in the American skinhead scene in the late 1980s.

The book *Skinhead* by Nick Knight is published.

1983   Most major American cities have a notable skinhead presence in their local punk scenes. Violence perpetrated by skinheads begins to become a problem in a few places, such as San Francisco. Youth Brigade releases its debut album, *Sound and Fury*, becoming the first Oi!-influenced American band to release an album.

Moon Records is found by Rob "Bucket" Hingley, frontman for the Toasters

The skinhead crew, Toehead Army emerges in the booming ska and mod revival scene in Los Angeles California

1984   Agnostic Front releases its first album, *Victim in Pain*.

Harley Flanagan forms the Cro-Mags.

Two skinheads in Chicago form a racist group called Romantic Violence, which is perhaps the first overtly racist skinhead group in the United States.

The Anti-Heroes group is formed in Atlanta. It will later become the most popular American Oi! band.

1985   Romantic Violence changes its name to CASH (Chicago Area Skin Heads).

American Front is formed in San Francisco, becoming the first racist skinhead crew in that city. Several incidents of violence connected to American Front members are reported in the city's Haight/Ashbury district.

Agnostic Front tours the United States for the first time, further spreading the skinhead concept around the country.

1986   The Cro-Mags release their first album, *The Age of Quarrel*, and tour the United States with English punk legends GBH.

New York skinheads appear on the *Phil Donahue Show*.

The Confederate Hammerskins are formed in Dallas, Texas.

1987   The second generation of American skinheads arrives.

The Anti-Heroes release their first album, *That's Right*, on England's Link Records. The group is the first pure U.S. Oi! band to release an album.

Incidents of racist skinhead violence are reported in the news in several cities such as San Jose, California, and Dallas, Texas.

The first chapter of WAR Skins is founded in Orange County, California.

The first chapter of Skinheads Against Racial Prejudice (SHARP) is founded in New York City.

1988   An edition of *The Oprah Winfrey Show* featuring skinheads is broadcast. The show makes news headlines the next day because of the tension between racist skinheads and antiracist skinheads and activists in the audience.

Racist skinhead activity increases dramatically in many cities, perhaps as a result of all the media exposure. This trend will continue for several more years.

The Bruisers are formed in Portsmouth, New Hampshire, They will become one of the most popular American Oi! bands of the late 1980s and early 1990s.

Warzone releases its debut album, *Don't Forget the Struggle, Don't Forget the Streets*.

The Hammerskin Nation is formed, bringing several different racist skinhead crews together under one umbrella. It will eventually have chapters in several European countries as well.

An infamous episode of *Geraldo* airs, in which the host's nose is broken during a melee involving Roy Innes and several racist skinheads and Tom Metzger.

Mulugeta Seraw is murdered in Portland, Oregon, by members of the racist skinhead gang called East Side White Pride.

1989   Minneapolis Baldies crew hosts a summit for antiracist organizations called the Syndicate, which 80 skinheads from Midwestern states attend.

Anti-Racist Action (ARA) is formed. It will eventually become a worldwide organization.

The U.S. Department of Justice establishes a skinhead taskforce within its civil rights division.

The Confederate Hammerskins have the distinction of being the first skinheads to be prosecuted under the enhanced hate crime legislation.

1990   The Anti-Heroes break up.

Patriot is formed in Chapel Hill, North Carolina. It will go on to become one of the most popular Oi! bands in the eastern United States.

The federal government passes the Hate Crimes Statistics Act, which authorizes the collection of data related to crimes based on religion, race, or sexual orientation.

The ska band Hepcat is formed.

1991   *Spirit of 69: Skinhead Bible* is published.

1992   The Templars are formed by drummer Phil Rigaud and singer/guitarist Carl Fritscher on Long Island, New York.

Oxblood is formed in New York City.

The first RASH chapter is formed in New Jersey.

1993   The Anti-Heroes re-form and soon reclaim their place at the top of the American Oi! scene.

United Front organizes a huge weekend festival in Washington, D.C., that brings together skinheads from around the country.

HBO's *Skinheads USA: Soldiers of the Race War* airs.

1994   The second United Front festival takes place but is marred by violence.

Pressure Point is formed in Sacramento, California. It becomes perhaps the best-known Oi! band in the Western United States.

The Templars release their first album, *The Return of Jacques de Molay.*

Popular British skinhead band the Business play their first show in the United States in New York City.

1995   The Anti-Heroes release the *American Pie* CD, which becomes one of the best-selling American Oi! recordings ever.

1996   The Dropkick Murphys form in Boston. They will become the most popular band to ever emerge from the American skinhead/Oi! scene.

The Beer Olympics festival is held in Atlanta. The festival, which is the brainchild of Mark Noah of the Anti-Heroes, becomes an annual event through 2002. This 2-day event features punk and Oi! bands from all over the United States.

1997   Warzone vocalist and legendary New York skinhead Ray Barbieri dies of pneumonia at the age of 35.

Skinheads.net is created by Chris Nutter.

1998   The ARA has an estimated 2,000 punk and skinhead members with chapters in 11 states, as well as in Germany and Colombia.

The book *American Skin* is published.

The film *American History X* is released.

2000   Moon Records closes its doors

2001   The Anti-Heroes break up. The Atlanta skinhead scene begins to decline in numbers.

2003   Skinhead numbers in many U.S. cities are noticeably lower than they were a few years earlier. The drop in numbers is noted among both racist and nonracist skinheads.

2006   The first East Coast Oi! Fest is held in Allentown, Pennsylvania, and features skinhead/Oi! bands from around the world.

The film *This Is England* is released in the United States.

The legendary club CBGB closes its doors.

2008   The third East Coast Oi! Fest is marred by a bottle-throwing melee between racist and nonracist skinheads.

Patriot re-forms, with an all new line-up alongside vocalist Eddie Oakes.

2009   A racist skinhead, Christoper Hawthorne, is shot and killed in San Diego, California, by an antiracist skinhead during an Oi! concert.

2010   Skinheads are once again in the news due to an assassination plot against President Barack Obama formulated by two members of the Supreme White Alliance from Tennessee.

An antiracist skinhead in Portland is shot and left for dead by members of the racist skinhead group Volksfront.

2011   David Lynch, founding member of American Front, is shot to death at home in Citrus Heights California.

Music festival 2000 Tons of TNT is held in Connecticut. The international lineup includes British bands Cockney Rejects and the Business as well as American skinhead bands Patriot, Broken Heroes, Hub City Stompers, Oxblood, and Immoral Discipline.

History of American Skinheads

Overview by Region

Even though the history of skinheads in the United States is less than 30 years old, the subculture has remained constant across the entire country since its inception. Skinheads did not manifest in just one city, but rather spread across multiple cities, with groups emerging around the country almost simultaneously. Regionally, certain cities and states contributed more to the growth and popularity of the skinhead subculture than others. In the Northeast, skinhead scenes were noted to exist since the early 1980s. The Midwest had the distinction of being the first area with skinhead gangs who espoused racist or antiracist ideology. The South was one of the later regions to fully develop skinhead scenes primarily in Florida and Georgia. The Southwest was dominated early on by racist skinhead gangs who were some of the first to form connections with groups such as the Ku Klux Klan. The West Coast had one of the largest skinhead populations, which spread from San Diego all the way to the Pacific Northwest cities of Seattle and Portland.

History by the Decades

The First U.S. Skinheads: 1980–1985

Harley Flanagan of the Cro-Mags at CBGB's last hardcore matinee, 2006 (Courtesy of Steven J. Messina).

Formation of the Subculture

Subcultures can be defined as groups of individuals who distinguish themselves from the social norm through music, hairstyles, dress, or some other means. Sociologist Kevin Mattson has argued that American youth subcultures of the 1980s differed from the corresponding British constructs due to the cultural differences between the United States and the United Kingdom. He asserts that to define a subculture, such as the punk subculture, solely based on its stylistic elements does not adequately consider the impact and formation of that movement.[1] The same can be said of American skinheads. While clothing and music constituted a major component of the subculture, politics and the "American way of life" eventually played a large part of what American youths defined as being a skinhead.

The first group of skinheads in the United States was found on the East Coast in 1980, with skinheads in Chicago and California arriving within the year. One of the first documented American-born skin-heads in the United States was Harley Flanagan, who became a key figure in the New York skinhead and hardcore scene. Sab Grey, who shaved his head in 1980, is credited with forming the first U.S. skin-head band, Iron Cross. In the Midwest, the first skinheads were found in Chicago in 1981. There were skinheads in Dallas as early as 1983, although their number was very small relative to the New York and California populations. San Francisco was also at the forefront of the skinhead subculture. Between 1980 and 1985, scores of skinheads could be found along Haight Street and at local punk venues. The ear-liest documented skinheads on the West Coast can be traced to 1981 in Southern California. Eventually the Bay Area became the home of the most notorious skinhead gangs, including the American Front and SF Skins, and the largest traditional skinhead scene in the nation.

With skinheads arriving in almost every major city by 1985, it was not long before significant populations of skinheads were found throughout the United States. As with any subculture, the sheer num-ber of youths affiliated with it led to inevitable regional variations and formation of scenes. Two distinct types of scenes were present in the early 1980s: hardcore skinheads and skinheads who, like British skin-heads, were associated with 2Tone music.

New York was perhaps the most significant city to shape the hard-core development of the subculture. In the early 1980s, skinheads were a regular sight on the Lower East Side of Manhattan. Popular hangout spots included Tompkins Square Park and the Hardcore Matinees at the club CBGB. The international flavor of New York was reflected in the diverse ethnic groups who made up a large part of the scene. Italians, Cubans, Puerto Ricans, and Blacks all embraced the subcul-ture, adopting the look of boots and braces and jeans.

While the New York hardcore scene was gaining momentum, a mirror scene was sprouting up in California. Hardcore skinheads emerged as an offshoot of the punk rock scene in both Northern and Southern California. Shawn Stern, from the band Youth Brigade, sported a shaved head, suspenders, and boots while still identifying himself as a punk. Other youths adopted the style and referred to themselves as skinheads.

At the same time that the hardcore skinhead scene started to grow in earnest, the 2Tone scene was also burgeoning in Southern

California. In the early days, these groups were relatively distinct. While they frequented some of the same areas, members of the two movements did not interact in a meaningful way until the growth of the Oi! scene and third wave Ska. As Martin, lead singer of the Oi! band Headstrong, recalls, "There were two strong skinhead scenes in LA in the 1980s, one in the punk scene and one in the Ska/mod scene, with some people crossing over." It was just as common for many first-generation skinheads to emerge from the Ska scene as from the hard-core punk scene.

Simultaneously, "hardcore skinheads" and skinheads who adopted their look from the 2Tone craze in the United Kingdom began showing up in various parts of California, including San Francisco, Sacramento, Fresno, Los Angeles, Hollywood, parts of Orange County, and even cities as remote as Palm Springs by 1983. During the initial appearance of the subculture, no one really took a conscious political side and the scene was more about skinhead music and American hardcore punk.

Skinhead Crews and Gangs

Within the spectrum of youth subcultures, there is typically a gradation of identification. While many youths identify as belonging to a larger group based on common interests, others adopt more extreme antisocial behaviors that categorize them as juvenile delinquents. Many skinheads fell into the latter category. While most of their delinquent activity was limited to vandalism, underage drinking, and fighting, skinheads gained a reputation for being antisocial and violent. This behavior meant skinheads quickly dominated local punk scenes and crews of skinheads formed as the population grew.

Membership in skinhead groups ranged from smaller crews having 6 to 10 members to larger crews with as many as 100 members. Crews are defined as loosely cohesive groups usually formed via friendships and the social affiliation of being a skinhead from a certain geographic area. Every large city had at least one crew, and some cities had multiple crews often fighting over the same areas. Eventually, some skinhead crews resembled the traditional youth gang structure. Gangs are typically defined by an initiation ritual, hierarchy of leadership, and frequent engagement in delinquent behavior for entertainment or economic profit.

Chicago had the distinction of being home to some of the first skinhead gangs in the United States. In 1982, the multiracial Bomber Boys formed; the flagship white supremacist gang Chicago Area Skinheads (CASH) followed within the year. Both crews spawned splinter groups with chapters of the Bomber Boys appearing in Atlanta and San Diego and CASH members inspiring the Confederate Hammerskins in Dallas and various other racist gangs.

The rise of the second-generation skinheads greatly increased the number of skinheads aligning themselves with established crews and gangs. With the proliferation of skinhead-related criminal behavior, law enforcement began tracking the development of the skinhead subculture. By the late 1980s, skinheads were treated like any other street gang, with their names and distinctive markings being cataloged by the police.

Second Generation of Skinheads: 1986–Present

The year 1986 marked the arrival of the second generation of skinheads. While the first generation was purely reliant on emulating the British subculture, the second generation of skinheads had an established scene to join. By 1986, the American version of the subculture was well defined, including clothing, music, and elder members who personified the skinhead image. Additionally, bands such as Warzone, Agnostic Front, Cro-Mags, and Murphy's Law popularized the culture of hardcore skinheads across the United States, and the distribution of skinhead music and clothing from England meant that these items began to be sold in specialty shops such as 99X in New York, Crash N Burn in Atlanta, and NaNas in Santa Monica.

Initially, all skinheads associated with one another regardless of politics. Over time, however, due to the growing division of the scene by racist rhetoric (namely, through racist British bands such as Skrewdriver and Brutal Attack), second-generation skinheads became more likely to consciously align themselves with an established crew or political ideology.

Racist and Antiracist Skinheads

In 1987, the police began to take notice of skinhead activity. Initially, they were not sure what to make of the skinhead subculture. In Portland,

Racist skinheads (AP Photo/Heribert Proepper).

Oregon, Captain Roberta Webber, commander of the Police Bureau's Central Precinct, acknowledged that "So much of the Skinheads' activity, at least from what I see, doesn't seem to be developed around the Nazi philosophy. It's more developed around music, a particular kind of music."[2] However, after a string of hate crimes were committed across the United States, this perspective among law enforcement changed.

By 1988, the skinhead scene was completely divided by racism. Some parts of the United States became strongholds for racist skinheads, whereas other cities became known for their antiracist skinheads. The most notorious racist gangs came from Illinois, Texas, Oklahoma, Florida, Oregon, and Northern California. While racist crews could be found across the nation, the groups in these cities rose to prominence for their criminal acts. Some skinhead groups began affiliating with other racist organizations such as the Aryan Nation and the Ku Klux Klan. Skinheads in Oklahoma City and Tulsa were among the first groups to affiliate themselves with paramilitary/survivalist extremist groups. Skinheads who did not subscribe to racism would openly fight with Nazis or grew their hair and got out of the scene altogether. The coverage of Nazi skinheads in the news gave them more leverage in recruiting new members to their groups. The overall sentiment of nonracist skinheads was similar to that of early skinhead Shawn Garard from the Washington, D.C., band Immoral Discipline: "Racist skinheads are new skins who pop up and do stupid things and give us all a bad name. They don't really understand the skinhead movement."[3]

In response to the increase in the number of racist skinheads, many states created anti-hate-crime legislation. Such laws led to a massive crackdown on skinhead gangs, including the Confederate Hammerskins in Texas, White Aryan Resistance Skins in California, and Chicago Area Skinheads in Illinois. Across the United States, racist skinheads were incarcerated and their crews became less of a threat. This trend contributed to the rise of traditional skinheads as the dominant strain of skinhead during the early to mid-1990s.

Traditional skinheads, Santa Cruz, California, 1986 (Courtesy of Chris Smith).

Rise of the Traditional Skinheads: 1990s

The term "traditional" was first used in the mid 1980s to differentiate skinheads who emulated first-generation British skinheads from those who were more influenced by the punk and Oi! movements. In the 1990s, the traditional skinhead style of music and fashion from England began to make an impact on most American skinhead scenes. One of the hallmarks of the traditional scene was that it was more stylistically diverse than the hardcore scene. The heart of the traditional scene was in the city of Santa Cruz in Northern California. While earlier skinheads in Los Angeles were considered traditional, the scene in Santa Cruz popularized the look for skinheads all over the United States. Plaid Ben Sherman shirts, wingtip brogue shoes, and tonic suits were added to the Northern California skinhead attire. In fact, other than having cropped hair, these individuals often did not resemble the Nazi skinheads whom people saw in the news.

During the 1990s, the hardcore and traditional skinhead subcultures diverged away from each other. The original hardcore skinhead scene gave way to early Oi! and Ska scenes in cities such as New York and San Francisco. While traditional skinheads started wearing Doc Martens, tapered jeans, braces, and flight jackets, hardcore style was more athletic and featured hooded sweatshirts and tennis shoes. Although the hardcore skins and the traditional skinheads in the cities dressed differently, most still associated with each other. As a New York skinhead named Frank recalls, "It was still a brotherhood of all types of skinheads."

The 2000s

By 2001, the skinhead subculture had begun to decline in prominence. There was waning interest in skinheads, and other subcultures such as punk, skater, and emo enjoyed greater popularity. Many third wave Ska and American Oi! bands broke up during this time; in turn, without music to bind them together, most scenes evaporated. Across the United States, skinheads began to trade in their boots and braces for other subcultures such as psychobilly or abandoned the scene altogether. In skinhead circles, the rockabilly scene was jokingly referred to as the "skinhead retirement plan."

By 2005, the subculture enjoyed a renaissance with the re-formation of original skinhead bands, the next wave of Ska music, and the advent of the Internet. The arrival of the Internet has ensured that the music, fashion, and interconnections among different scenes remain strong. The Internet has also allowed skinheads from across the country to interact virtually via message boards and social networks.

The skinhead subculture is still in existence in all major U.S. cities. The original cities that contributed to the formation of the subculture no longer play such prominent roles in its ongoing life, however. Within the scenes that are still active, traditional and hardcore skinheads represent the majority of participants; although, racist skinheads have been documented by law enforcement in most states within the last 5 years. The line between hardcore skinheads and traditional skinheads has blurred, such that an observer is just as likely to see both types of skinheads at the same shows. Regionally, different types of skinheads are found in varying concentrations. Although there are no recent demographic statistics, the skinhead social website Skinheads.net boasts 8,000 members, which is an indicator of the current population's size. The Anti-Defamation League of B'nai B'rith (ADL) documented 110 racist skinhead groups in 2006. According to the ADL website, *Racist Skinhead Project*, 10 assaults attributed to racist skinhead gangs occurred in that year, almost exclusively in the West and Pacific Northwest regions of the United States.[4]

Some areas are still known for being antiracist or White Power strongholds; in these areas, members of the two groups rarely cross the other's boundaries. When the two groups have interacted, deadly consequences have ensued. For example, three deaths in Southern California were attributed to clashes between Nazis and antiracist crews between 2008 and 2010.

Currently, the largest skinhead population on the East Coast is found in North Carolina. New York City is home to a small skinhead population, but it is no longer the epicenter of the subculture that it once was.

Farther south, the Atlanta scene is a shell of its former self. Although skinheads still live there, compared to the heyday of the late 1980s and 1990s the scene is all but dead. While the Color Blind Crew (CBC) is active in southern Florida, there is an equally active chapter of Confederate Hammerskins in central Florida.

Today the largest skinhead scenes in the Southwest are all located in Texas. Houston and San Antonio have the largest crews, along with bands to support the growth of the scene. Skinheads in these city comprise a predominately Hispanic population, reflective of the larger demographics of the cities. A small scene exists in Phoenix, Arizona, as well. Traditional and hardcore skinheads are in the majority in the region; however, racist skinheads have been documented by law enforcement in all of the Southwest states within the last 5 years.

On the West Coast, the skinhead subculture in the Los Angeles area is still lively, featuring regularly scheduled concerts and reggae nights. Although most gangs are inactive, music shows continue to be marred by violence.

In the Pacific Northwest, the Rose City Bovver Boys dominate the traditional skinhead scene. This group is one of the only nonracist crews left in the city of Portland and celebrated its 15-year anniversary in 2009.

Conversely, Volksfront has the largest presence in the Pacific Northwest in the White Power scene. This group's members were recently featured in the television series *Gangland*. Volksfront has chapters across the United States as well as in Europe. The Southern Poverty Law Center identifies it as one of the largest skinhead hate groups still active in America.

Notes

1. Kevin Mattson, "Did Punk Matter? Analyzing the Practices of a Youth Subculture During the 1980s," *American Studies* 42, no. 1 (Spring 2001): 69–97.
2. "No Accurate Estimate of Genuine Skinheads Is Possible, Say Police," *Seattle Times* (Seattle, WA) (December 27, 1987): B6.
3. James Rupert, "Beatings Said to Reflect Dark Side of 'Skinheads,'" *Washington Post* (December 19, 1988): Metro, E1.
4. Anti-Defamation League of B'nai B'rith Racist Skinhead Project, accessed November 12, 2010, http:/www.adl.org/racist_skinheads/.

Becoming a Skinhead

Since the inception of the subculture, scholars in both England and the United States have attempted to categorize and decipher why youths decide to become skinheads. Books such as *The Paint House: Words from an East End Gang* by Susie Daniel et al. in 1972, and *Subculture: The Meaning of Style* by Dick Hebdige in 1979, provided insight into the first generation of the subculture.

In examining the skinhead phenomenon in America, sociological and criminological theories have been used to explain why thousands of youths have shaved their heads in the United States. Scholars have examined the subculture primarily using theories of social deviance. Skinheads have been characterized as gangs and even terrorist organizations. From this body of research, the overall emergence of the skinheads has been attributed to some combination of the following factors: economic status, social class, social deviance, aggression, and alienation.

The skinhead subculture is first and foremost a youth cult. Researchers have found the average age of youths who become skinheads is usually between 14 and 16. The average duration for which a youth "claims" or labels himself or herself a skinhead is 6 years. For this reason, the transition into "becoming" a skinhead is grounded in adolescent

Michigan skinhead, 1998 (Courtesy of Jacob Fuller).

development and other rites of passage common in various youth movements. As with other subcultures, youths are attracted to the skinhead life for a variety of reasons. In turn, when asked how they became skinheads, the answers vary. Doug, a California skinhead, remembers, "In 1981, they broadcast the story of the Southhall riots at my high school. After that I was hooked." Ted, from San Francisco, recalls, "I was 14 and a lonely little runt looking for something to belong to."

Skinhead youths are typically involved in other subcultures before becoming skinheads. For example, researcher Randy Blazak found that 85 percent of skinheads in his study identified as being involved in other specific subcultures before becoming skinheads.[1] While this trend varies by region, being a skateboarder or a punk is the most common gateway to becoming a skinhead. Other subcultures identified as preceding membership in the skinhead subculture include the mod, metal, and scooter scenes.

Danny Oi, Portland, 1992 (Coyote Days)

Another way youths find out about the existence of skinheads is through family members and friends. Andy Anthrax, a skinhead from Texas, says, "I first found out about skinhead in 1984 from my brother, who had been a skinhead since 1983. Before that I used to listen to punk rock and metal music."

Family Life

Skinheads come from all types of families and socioeconomic backgrounds. Skinheads in the United States tend to differ from British youths in that they are as likely to come from the middle class as from the working class. Some skinheads have stable home lives, contrary to the commonly held view of skinheads as "alienated, disaffected youth who come from dysfunctional family backgrounds."[2] Cliff, an early skinhead from Southern California, recalls, "I had a suburban upbringing, you know a good Christian household, and my parents didn't mind that I was a skinhead, at all." Of course, not all skinheads come from nuclear families. Some skinheads have grown up in the projects in Chicago and New York, lived on the streets, and came from broken homes. Although a disproportionate number of skinheads are children of divorce, their family situations are not the sole factor driving them to choose the skinhead lifestyle.

Skinheads and Identity Formation

Skinheads are generally part of a "scene," which is defined as a central location usually focused on music or other social events that are commonly identified as part of the "skinhead lifestyle." Scenes are loosely formed, with the population constantly fluctuating between the core set of skinheads and those who socialize with them and are either from the same region or farther away.

As with many street cultures, skinheads form and re-form connections. In this very transient subculture, it is not uncommon for skinheads to move from one city to another depending on the size or popularity of the scene. For example, the skinhead scene in Atlanta, Georgia, was affected greatly both in size and in style by transplants from places such as Chicago, New York, and Los Angeles. Through the scene and the connections between friends and acquaintances, skinhead culture is transmitted from individuals and groups. Each scene varies by region and size, depending on how robust the commitment of its members is and how many social events occur. A major factor influencing the vitality of a scene is how many bands perform regularly in the area. The bigger the local music scene, the larger a skinhead population will grow. Likewise, the decline of a music scene correlates with the shrinking and, in some cases, total disappearance of a scene.

Skinhead Ritual

Becoming a skinhead involves more than just adopting the outer guise of a skinhead by shaving one's head and putting on skinhead-influenced clothing. Part of becoming a skinhead includes associating with other skinheads, proving your authenticity, and being able to embody skinhead values. One cannot be a skinhead without becoming involved in a scene and gaining respect from other skinheads.

Authenticity

One of the main ways to become a skinhead is to be authentic. Authenticity takes place when one befriends other skinheads, then proves one's value as a skinhead by sticking up for friends and being genuine. Frank from the band Oxblood says of being a skinhead, "Be true to yourself and stand your ground no matter what—whether you win or lose." Additionally, being knowledgeable about the history of the skinhead subculture and lifestyle is important for developing credibility. It is not uncommon for youths who decide to adopt the skinhead lifestyle to wait until they know other skinheads before they shave their head. Some scenes have unwritten rules about when and how someone can be "shaved in." Pan, a Portland (Oregon) skinhead, notes, "I hung out with skinheads for a year before I shaved my head and dressed like a skin." Likewise, length of time in the scene and the number of people with whom a person associates affects the individual's sense of legitimacy in a scene. "Even if you wear the clothes, know the music, and call yourself a skin, if you are not authentic, you are not considered a skinhead."

Respect

As skinheads became firmly rooted in America and the first generation gave way to a second one, respect became another important prerequisite to entering into an already developed scene. Many times, respect is one of the main reasons why someone is expelled or never fully accepted into a skinhead scene. When a skinhead is a "freshcut" or new to a city, that individual must prove his or her legitimacy by respecting the members of that community.

Violence

Another prevalent theme of the skinhead subculture is violence. As Phil, drummer for the skinhead band The Templars, observes, "Fighting is something that comes with the uniform. If you were a skinhead who

Jesse, skinhead girl, New Orleans, 2007 (Kelly Hardy).

didn't fight, you were pathetic and you get beat down or weren't a skinhead for very long." Like other subcultures centered on aggression, fighting is a regular part of the skinhead lifestyle. It is a source of legitimacy
and a way to earn respect. For some skinheads, violence is a source of
gratification and often the lure that draws youths to the subculture in
the first place. It is rare to find a skinhead who has never been in a fight
at some time in his or her life. This sentiment is echoed in the words of
Marty, an Indiana skin: "Skinhead was the best time of my life—the
music, the violence, the blue collar backgrounds. I really liked the violence—thrived on it. It was an escape from everyday life." One skinhead
girl acknowledges, "I used to fight before I was a skinhead so it was nothing new—if there wasn't fighting in skinhead, it wouldn't be nearly as

---

Authenticity: "If one is unable to display authentic characteristics,
they are often dismissed by the scene and ostracized. But to be a
skinhead there's a minimum baseline of honor and morality."

—Grover, skinhead, Cincinnati

fun." Blazak found that 100 percent of skinheads surveyed responded "yes" to the question, "Is it ever OK to punch an adult male stranger?"[3]

Skinhead Attitude

Skinhead identity emphasizes pride in self and country. There are several ideals that virtually all skinheads seek to uphold: pride, nationalism, working class ethic, loyalty, and unity.

Pride and nationalism are among the main tenets of skinhead identity. In England, skinhead nationalism was seen as a backlash against immigrants who entered the country after World War II, but in America it was interpreted as patriotism. Skinheads would put American flag patches on their flight jackets to display their country allegiance. The large number of skinheads joining the military reflects this desire to display patriotism by fighting for one's country.

The concept of pride also carries over in the way an individual skinhead presents himself or herself. Polished boots and a clean-cut appearance are the standard. Skinheads often speak disparagingly of the punk scene that by the 1980s adopted the "crusty punk" look, where pan-handling and disheveled, ripped clothing were the norms.

The laudatory attitude toward the working class as a core value of the skinhead subculture can be traced directly to England. While U.K. skinheads were predominantly working-class citizens, American skinheads, who came from all social classes, soon redefined the term "working class." The American skinhead definition of the working class more closely mirrors the "pull yourself up by your bootstraps" belief system characteristic of the Reagan era of the 1980s. As a result, American skinheads define the working class as individuals who work for what they have as opposed to having everything handed to them.

Traditional: Listens to both Oi! music and 1960s reggae. Members of this group emulate first- and second-generation British skinheads. The term "traditional" and "trad" was born out of the need to distinguish these individuals from racist skinheads. Purists in this category listen solely to reggae and soul and dress in vintage clothing.

> **Racist:** Listens to racist and other types of Oi! music. Members of this group label themselves as White Pride or White Power skinheads. Initially these skinheads did not subscribe to specific racial doctrines; however, by 1988 many identified with established hate groups. Most skinheads do not consider racism to be part of the skinhead subculture.

The term "unity" is often used as a synonym for "pride" and "loyalty" by skinheads. All of these qualities are deemed important attributes of the skinhead subculture. The concept of unity applies to both male and female skinheads. In an interview, Raymond "Raybeez" Barbieri, singer for the skinhead band Warzone, described the New York scene as follows: "The Lower East Side Crew is a very big family of skin guys and girls. . . . We are all very close, like brothers and sisters."[4] It is not uncommon for skinheads to describe their bonds with one another in terms of family or brotherhood. Another New York skinhead band, Agnostic Front, titled its first release *United Blood*. That sense of connection—of belonging—is another reason why youths gravitate toward this subculture.

These core values have remained the same across the more than 30 years of the skinhead subculture's existence. By tracing the history of the skinhead movement across the various regions of the United States, it becomes evident that the skinhead subculture has maintained a strong presence among American youth.

Common Categories of Skinheads

As the subculture was refined and grew in the United States, several types of skinheads evolved from the original skinheads of the early

> **Antiracist:** Musical tastes and clothing style range from traditional to hardcore. This category arose as a backlash against the growth of White Power skinheads. While many skinheads are nonracist, antiracist skinheads are willing to organize and engage in violence to eradicate racist elements from their scene.

Political: Musical tastes and clothing style range from traditional to hardcore. This type of skinhead adopts a particular political stance ranging from human rights to communism. As is the case with racism, many skinheads do not consider political values to be part of the skinhead subculture and look down on political activism in the scene.

Hardcore: Listens to hardcore music and is heavily influenced by punk. Hardcore skinheads follow the most casual form of skinhead style with T-shirts, jeans, and boots. This group can be characterized as the most Americanized version of skinheads, as they incorporate very few elements of first- or second-generation British skinheads into their lifestyle.

Oi Boys: Listen to Oi! music and are influenced by the second generation of British skinheads. They are often the stereotyped image portrayed in popular culture, wearing flight jackets, jeans, boots, and braces. Most often, they do not listen to 1960s reggae music, preferring the harder sound of street rock and hardcore.

1980s. Sociologists have defined the skinhead subculture as a group of individuals who subscribe to a set of definitions regarding physical appearance, musical interests, and lifestyle. While there is no single label that can be placed on every skinhead, these are certain basic characteristics that one may observe in any given scene. These definitions are neither all-inclusive nor absolute, and in many cases skinheads do not consider themselves to fit in a particular category. In her dissertation on American skinheads, Dr. Sylvia Sievers notes, "Although various factions are often distinct in their political values and differentiate themselves along specific boundaries, their outward appearance and their investment in the skinhead identity tie them together under one label known as 'skinhead.'"[5]

Notes

1. Randy Blazak, *The Suburbanization of Hate: An Ethnographic Study of the Skinheads Subculture* (Ph.D. dissertation, Emory University, 1995), 111.

2. Jennifer Lynn Bard, *An Exploratory Analysis of Youth in Skinhead Groups* (M.A. thesis, Simon Fraser University, Canada, 1999), 27.

3. Randy Blazak, *The Suburbanization of Hate: An Ethnographic Study of the Skinheads Subculture* (Ph.D. dissertation, Emory University, 1995), 92.

4. Interview, unidentified fanzine, 1987.

5. Sylvia Jane Sievers, *American Skinheads: An Investigation into the Acquisition of a Deviant Identity* (Ph.D. dissertation, State University of New York at Stony Brook, 2003).

| # Skinhead Fashion

The original roots of skinhead dress derive from the rudeboy and mod subcultures of 1960s England. British skinheads were later influenced by the style of punk. Skinhead fashion in America has always been somewhat different than its British counterpart. When skinheads first arrived in the United States, their entry coincided with the late 1970s and early 1980s skinhead revival in England. The skinhead subculture was very influenced by punk in terms of both music and fashion. This link was even stronger in America, where the skinhead subculture was viewed as an extension of the punk rock scene. In 1980, American skinheads were basically bald punk rockers. They wore leather jackets, flannel shirts, and other items that were not part of the traditional skinhead uniform.

By 1983, American skinheads were doing their best to emulate the styles they saw on album covers and books such as *Skinhead* by Nick Knight. However, typical British skinhead clothing items were very difficult—if not impossible—to find in most U.S. cities. Doc Marten boots were available in only a handful of punk specialty shops such as Poseur in Hollywood and 99th Floor in Chicago. U.S. Army boots were commonly worn instead. Fred Perry polo shirts were even more difficult to come by, as were Ben Sherman dress shirts and thin suspenders. Some skinheads in Chicago and San Francisco went so far as to make their own suspenders using elastic and mitten clips. Instead of British brands, American skinheads wore other dress shirt labels such as Arrow or Gant and Ralph Lauren polo shirts because they were easier to find and did not come with import (i.e., more expensive) prices. In an odd twist, many of the items British skinheads wore were American staples such as Levi's and U.S. bomber flight jackets. Much of the most prized clothing, however, was available only in the United Kingdom.

When skinhead numbers started growing substantially in the mid-1980s, more shops started to cater to this population's music and clothing needs. As a result, more American skinheads resembled their British counterparts. The harder punk-influenced Oi! style of second-generation skinheads was copied more than the original style of the late 1960s.

By this time, American skinheads were also very much influenced by the hardcore scene. Hardcore style was largely based on athletic apparel: baggy jeans or shorts, sneakers, "wife-beater" tank tops, oversized T-shirts, and hooded sweatshirts.

By the early 1990s, the original "traditional" British skinhead style had become more popular among American skinheads. For the first time, large numbers of skinheads were discovering the style and music of the 1960s. This trend was due in large part to the book *Spirit of '69*, which was published in 1991. It included a comprehensive chapter on traditional skinhead style, complemented by pictures, and its content served as a model for many new skinheads. Before the book was published, fanzines based on traditional skinhead subculture featured images of skinheads from the late 1960s and fashion tips. For some participants in this movement, skinhead fashion became an important source of pride, and they took great care to project the image of original skinheads from England.

Skinhead girls have often been said to look just as masculine as their male counterparts. In many cases, they have been more limited in their fashion choices than girls in other subcultures. The evolution of clothing for skinhead girls has been most marked in the last decade. In the early 1980s, American skinhead girls dressed like skinhead males or wore punk clothing. By the late 1980s, the traditional style incorporated skirts and fishnet tights and more feminine pieces. Nevertheless, skinhead girls were still largely limited to male clothing. It was common for smaller girls to buy boys' shirts or size small men's shirts. By the mid-1990s, the most desired clothes were available through mail order from the United Kingdom, however, and companies in the United States started to create clothing for skinhead girls.

The skinhead "uniform" varies regionally, although certain key elements are accepted universally. The following is a brief overview of skinhead style components.

Hairstyles

Hair is the most distinctive aspect of the skinhead subculture. Not only is the name of the movement derived from the hairstyle, but it has long been a noticeable difference between skinheads and the other

Fringe haircut and sideburns—typical skinhead styles, 1985 (Chris Schaefer).

related subcultures of mods and punks. Most original U.S. skinheads either shaved their heads completely or had a #1 guard crop. Facial hair of any kind was not acceptable.

By the mid-1980s, a #1 or #2 crop became the norm and sideburns called "chops" started to appear as more American skinheads became aware of the style. Facial hair also helped define the subculture. Facial hair varies among the different skinhead subgroups. Clean shaven with sideburns is the standard for traditional skinhead fashion, but goatees have become acceptable in some scenes, especially White Power ones. This preference persisted throughout the 1990s and continues today. Some skinheads wear their hair as long as a #3 or #4 crop, but anything longer is not considered to qualify as a skinhead style. In England, as skinheads grew their hair, they were referred to as Suedeheads or Smoothies. While the grown-out style was prevalent in the 1990s in Northern California, it was not typical of the rest of the American skinhead population.

Skinhead girl hairstyles are usually shorter on top with longer hair on the sides and back. Three distinct types of hairstyles fit within this general principle: the Chelsea, the fringe, and the feathercut.

The Chelsea is the American term for the classic skinhead girl haircut and is the first cut most girls get when they become part of

Feathercuts—a popular haircut for skinhead girls (Courtesy of oldhcdude).

the skinhead cult. It is defined as a very short crop, made with a blade ranging from #1 to a #3 guard, with two longer pieces on the sides and short bangs in front. This was the dominant hairstyle among American skinhead girls throughout the 1980s and 1990s in most areas, with the exception of California, where the largest population of traditional skinheads during that era favored the fringe.

The fringe is another common style. With this style, the top is a short, #2 or #3 guard crop, with short to long bangs and longer pieces all around the face and the back of the head.

Perhaps the most feminine looking is the feathercut. In this style, the hair is worn longer on top than in the Chelsea or fringe but is still shorter than the sides. Bangs are worn longer as well, and the hair is longest on the sides and back. This hairstyle is usually worn by skinhead girls who have been involved in the skinhead scene for a number of years. Older skinhead women opted for this less severe style, especially when assimilating into society.

Tops

Fred Perry tennis shirts and Ben Sherman button-down dress shirts are British brand shirts. In the United States, these shirts are the preferred items for skinheads, along with T-shirts in warmer climates. Fred Perry polo shirts are made in solid colors as well as with different color piping around the collar and sleeves. Fred Perry dress shirts are also worn, but remain difficult to find in the United States. Ben Sherman makes many different styles of shirts as well as other types of clothing, but classic skinhead shirts have long or short sleeves with a button-down collar and a pleat in the back. Traditional style dictates that short-sleeve

---

Fred Perry: Fred Perry is best known as the last English tennis player to win the Wimbledon men's championship in 1938. In 1952, he started a brand of tennis shirts under his name. In the 1960s, Fred Perry shirts were worn by mods and skinheads, and have remained a staple of the skinhead style ever since.

Ben Sherman: Ben Sherman is a clothing company founded in 1963 by Arthur Bernard Sugarman. It is the fourth largest British casual wear company, producing shirts, shoes, suits, sweaters, and various accessories. Mods were the first subculture to wear Ben Sherman's line of button-down shirts, and skinheads followed suit in the late 1960s.

Ben Shermans should have a V-cut in the sleeve in the hem of a sleeve, with a button on top. Both brands have seen a surge in their commercial success, which has helped with their U.S. distribution. Ben Sherman has opened stores in major cities, and Fred Perry clothing is sold in national retail outlets. Vintage U.K. brands such as Brutus and Jaytex are also sought after by skinhead purists. In addition to polos and button-ups, T-shirts with band logos are very popular.

Fred Perry V-neck sweaters are considered a skinhead standard. The most commonly worn colors are black, maroon, navy, and gray. Sweaters are typically worn over button-down dress shirts. Cardigans were worn in the early 1990s but are rarely seen on American skinheads these days.

Hooded and crew-neck sweatshirts are worn by hardcore skinheads but are not considered part of the traditional style. As with T-shirt brands such as Lonsdale, band logos are often seen on hardcore sweatshirts.

Bottoms

Denim jeans are without a doubt the most common pants worn by skinheads. The preferred brand is Levi's straight-leg 501s, but 505s and 550s are also acceptable. Other brands, such as Lee and Wrangler, are considered suitable as well, albeit only in straight-leg and relaxed styles. For skinhead purists, Levi's Sta-Prest trousers are prized possessions, as they were popular among original skinheads. Many U.S. skinheads wear American working-class brands such as Dickies and Ben Davis. The styles of these pants consist of a front-cut chino style in black, khaki, charcoal, or green. Army Battle Dress Uniform (BDU) pants are worn as well, in both the plain and camouflage versions;

however, this attire is more common among hardcore and White Power skinheads.

Mini-skirts are universally preferred bottoms among skinhead girls. Denim skirts and plain colors such as black, red, navy, gray, and olive green are standard. Plaid miniskirts are a style adopted from punk. Skirts are usually worn with fishnet stockings.

Jackets and Coats

U.S. Air Force MA1 flight jackets (more simply, "flight jackets") are probably the most favored type of jacket among skinheads today. Black and green are trendy colors, but maroon and navy blue are worn as well. Harrington jackets are considered traditional and are also available in many different colors. Denim and corduroy jackets—especially Levi's red-tag denim and white tag corduroy jackets—are skinhead classics. Mod parkas, sheepskin coats, and donkey jackets are sometimes worn by skinheads who live in colder climates. Three-quarter-length Crombie overcoats are fashionable nighttime dress wear.

Tonic suits worn by traditional skinheads, 1990 (Courtesy of Michele Alaniz).

Suits

Traditional skinheads wear suits for special occasions. They are the ultimate dress wear for a night of dancing to reggae and soul. Single-breasted three-button suits with straight-leg trousers are the norm. They are usually paired with wing-tip shoes or loafers. Houndstooth and Prince-of-Wales checked suits are highly prized, and expensive, skinhead fashion items. Currently, the most desired fabric is a three ply mohair cloth called Tonik created by the British fabric company Dormeuil in 1956. The two tone sheen of the fabric was unique and much sought after by original skinheads and came in black, navy, gray, or maroon. This style of fabric was later copied and manufactured by other companies and became known as "tonic." In the 1980s, American skinheads would find tonic suits in thrift stores, as they were common in the 1950s and 1960s. The cut and style of these items were then altered to resemble the cut popular among English skinheads. Girls would take large tonic pants and have them recut into skirts. Today specialty clothiers in England make reproductions of tonic suits for both men and women.

Footwear

Dr. Marten Boots, also referred to as "docs" or "DMs," are the brand of footwear most closely associated with skinheads the world over, and the United States is no exception. References to these boots appear in both songs and skinhead terminology. For example, the terms "bootboys," "bootgirls," and "boot party" are references to skinheads and Doc Martens. This footwear became the standard among British skinheads because of Doc Martens' status as workmen's boots. At the time of their introduction in England, they quickly gained a reputation for their comfort and high style based on their air-cushioned soles and the ability to polish the leather. In the United States, Doc Martens have never been associated with anything other than fashion. The eight-hole 1460 boot is a classic of the original skinhead era. Ten- and fourteen-hole boots became the norm in the 1980s among both punks and skinheads.

Doctor Marten boots (Courtesy of Chris Smith).

Eight- and ten-hole Doc Martens are the most widely worn; anything higher is frowned upon by skinhead purists. Black and oxblood red are the preferred colors, although brown is also considered acceptable. The same preferences apply to the three-hole shoes. Steel-toe boots and shoes are most commonly worn, but soft-toe footwear is still popular.

Monkey Boots were another style that was seen in the 1980s, especially among younger skinhead girls and boys, as originally Doc Martens were not available in smaller sizes in the United States.

Today Grinders shoes and boots have taken over a lot of the American skinhead market from Dr. Marten Boots. Although they are heavier than Doc Martens and, therefore, not as comfortable, they are better made and last longer. Again, eight- and ten-hole boots are the norm, with the three-hole shoes being very popular as well. Black, oxblood, and antique are the preferred colors. Paramilitary style boots with heavy screw-in soles are worn as well, but seem to be more common among White Power skinheads. Gripfast, Gladiator, and Underground are the most popular brands among today's skinheads.

Men's dress shoes like Brogues and Loafers with tassels or penny slots are commonly worn by skinheads, especially with suits. Loafers are worn more by skinhead girls than by their male counterparts. To

> **Dr. Martens:** Dr. Martens is a brand of workboot developed by Dr. Klaus Maertens in 1945. In 1960, a British shoemaker bought the manufacturing rights and changed the name to Dr. Martens. By the late 1960s, these boots had become popular among skinheads; they have been associated with the subculture ever since.

mimic this style, Dr. Marten manufactured both loafers and wing-tipped brogues with AirWare soles which became a favorite of traditional skinheads in the 1990s.

In cities with large hardcore scenes, athletic shoes were accepted in the subculture. While Adidas were worn by skinheads since the late 1970s and 1980s in the UK, it is only within the last 15 years that Adidas Samba soccer shoes have become preferred in the United States, thanks to the popularity of soccer among skinheads.

Braces and Laces

Braces—or suspenders, as they are usually called in the United States—are either ½ or ¾ inch wide when worn as part of skinhead attire; anything wider than 1 inch is considered unfashionable. The proper braces frequently have to be ordered from the United Kingdom, as suspenders this thin are difficult to find elsewhere. British braces tend to be of higher quality than anything made in the United States. Black, maroon, red, gray, and white are the principal colors. Plaid and striped patterns were worn in the 1980s, but today they are not considered proper skinhead style.

Shoelaces also come in a variety of colors. Black laces are standard in all brands of shoes and boots, but many skinheads replace them with red, white, and yellow versions. Different meanings have been attached to the color of laces that a skinhead chooses to wear in his boots since the early days of the American skinhead scene. Some of these relationships have an element of truth attached to them, whereas others are simply myths. Lace codes have always been more prevalent among White Power skinheads, but some nonracist and antiracist skinheads and crews have used them as well. To confuse things even further, the same color could have a completely different meaning

Lace Codes:

Red: White Power, Nazi, skinhead has spilled blood for his or her race. Could also stand for communist or "red-skin."

White: White Power, White Pride. Some antiracist skinheads wore one black lace and one white lace to symbolize racial unity.

Black: No special meaning.

Yellow: "Police killer."

Blue: Ultra-violence.

depending on the city or geographic area. Lace codes were much more common in the 1980s and early 1990s than today. Most nonracist skinheads attach no meaning to the color of their boot-laces; that is, the color is a matter of personal taste and nothing more.

Casual and Leisure Attire

American skinheads have created a new division of fashion in the skinhead subculture, primarily through the explosion of the hardcore scene and its influence on skinheads worldwide. U.S. skinheads also have brought a more relaxed set of rules in terms of neatness to the subculture. This can be explained in several ways. The United States has many different types of climates, from subarctic to tropical. Some areas, such as the Midwest, have very cold winters and hot summers, requiring a much wider range of clothing than one would find in the United Kingdom.

Shorts are customarily seen on skinheads during the summer; Dickies and Army-style ones are common. Army shorts are often

Gangster Style: Los Angeles skinheads became notorious for the rise of "gangsta skinhead style," which was a hybrid of traditional skinhead and street gang clothing. The style consisted of Dickies, white "wife-beater" tank tops, and cloth shoes called winos. An L.A. skinhead explained, "It was more a financial thing than a fashion thing."

White Power Skinhead Style: In the 1980s, racist skinheads dressed like most other skinheads. By the 1990s, however, their look bore little resemblance to traditional skinhead style. It evolved into a mix of hardcore and military style with BDU pants, T-shirts, boots, and flight jackets, which are adorned with racist symbols to designate Nazi affiliation.

BDU pants cut to the desired length, typically just below the knee. Shirts are sometimes worn untucked in hot weather. Wife-beaters are frequently worn as well. Shoes are accepted in lieu of boots. Grinders with three eyelets, Doc Marten 1461s, and Adidas Sambas are the most popular styles.

Shirts with racist logos—commonly worn by Nazi skinheads (AP Photo/Carolyn Kaster).

Tattoos

Tattoos are increasingly standard among skinheads. In fact, tattoos are one of the easiest ways to tell the differences between different types of skinheads. In some cities, it is considered a rite of passage to get a skinhead-related tattoo. Some tattoos must be "earned," especially if they are gang related.

Common designs among traditional and Oi! skinheads are the crucified skin (a skinhead depicted on a cross, as the name implies), Trojan helmet, Doc Marten boots, and the Fred Perry laurel wreath emblem. Traditional American tattoo styles such as brass knuckles, pin-up girls, justice scales, and slogans like "Don't Tread on Me" and "Man's Ruin" are popular among all types of skinheads as well.

Skinheads' tattooed inside lip (Courtesy of oldhcdude).

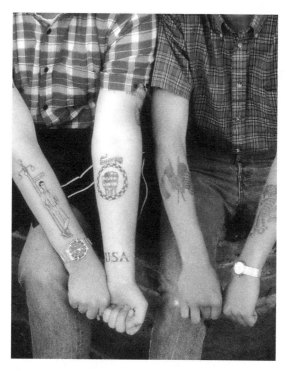

Skinhead tattoos (Courtesy of Chris Smith).

Tattoo designs frequently observed among racist skinheads included SS lightning bolts, Celtic crosses, runes, Viking and Nordic warriors like Thor and Odin, crossed hammers, and the swastika. Racist slogans such as 88 ("h" is the eighth letter of the alphabet, so 88 stands for "Heil Hitler"), 14-words, and WPWW ("White Pride World-Wide") are common tattoos among White Power skinheads.

Mail Order and the Internet

Since the turn of the century, the Internet has revolutionized the way American skinheads shop for clothes, and there is now an unprecedented variety of items available to them. Previously, skinheads had to rely on hand-me-downs or buy gear from skinheads who were getting out of the scene. With the advent of the Internet, however, skinheads now have direct access to distributors and individuals all over the world selling clothing and accessories. Online bidding sites such as

Racist tattoos (AP Photo/Ann Johansson).

eBay have been a boon to those skinheads who live in less populated areas and/or are on a budget. Many mail-order sites aimed at the skinhead market have started up worldwide over the past few years, and Paypal and credit cards have made purchasing items easier. Some of the more popular sites are Crash and Burn in Atlanta, as well as Warrior Clothing and the Merc, both of which operate out of England.

Skinhead-Run Clothing Companies

Several clothing companies run by skinheads or persons closely connected to the skinhead subculture have started up in recent years. They include Modern-action in San Francisco, which offers a line of button-down shirts at more moderate prices than Ben Sherman or Fred Perry. The shirts come in both long and short sleeves and in a variety of patterns: plain, plaid, and gingham check. The material and tailoring are both top quality. Hammersmith Clothing is a mail-order company from New York City run by Carl Fritscher, that offers T-shirts, hooded sweatshirts, and polo shirts in guys and girls styles, as well as Harrington jackets. Fritscher's reason for starting the company was simple: "I noticed there were no companies in the U.S. making skinhead clothes."

While some skinheads do not focus on style as a major part of their lifestyle, a large portion of the—pays great care and attention to the details of their clothing as an integral part of being a skinhead.

| # Skinhead Music in the United States

The first generation of skinheads in England listened to 1960s Jamaican reggae, whose sound was characterized by a catchy fusion of Caribbean rhythms and American jazz. Jamaican imports such as *Israelites* by Desmond Dekker and the Aces topped the charts in the United Kingdom in 1969. The music was so popular that in the late 1970s British youth created their own version of reggae called 2Tone. It was a blend of the original 1960s Ska infused with the fast-tempo energy of punk. The music, which was named for its blend of black and white musical sounds, represented a reaction to the rise of the conservative political group the National Front.

The 2Tone movement in the United Kingdom was largely responsible for the resurgence of the skinhead subculture in the late 1970s. The music of bands such as Madness, The Specials, English Beat, and The Selecter swept across England with infectious Ska beats and soulful melodies. Some of their songs were covers of early reggae tunes, and their look was heavily influenced by the original style of mods and skinheads. Other bands, such as the Bodysnatchers and Bad Manners, further rounded out the 2Tone movement.

The second generation of skinheads also gravitated to a style of punk called Oi! Oi! is characterized by cleaner guitars and slower

The Specials, 1980 (Photo by Fred Hermansky/NBCU Photo Bank via AP Images).

tempos than most punk music, and many Oi! songs feature sing-along, "soccer chant" choruses. The music produced by bands such as Sham 69, Angelic Upstarts, Cockney Rejects, Cock Sparrer, and the 4skins reflected the anger and working-class ethic that characterized what it was to be a skinhead. It is important to keep in mind that Oi! music originated in England and that American skinheads listened to those bands. As Harley Flanagan recalls, "We were aware of what was going on over there and it was influencing bands like Iron cross from [Washington,] D.C., Agnostic Front from NYC, and even early Cro-Mags songs with sing-along anthems."[1]

Skinhead music in the United States can be traced back to 1980 with the formation of Iron Cross in Washington, D.C. The earliest adopters of the traditional Oi! sound were New Jersey's U.S. Chaos with their first album *We've Got the Weapons* released in 1983. Because of the vast number of bands that have come and gone on the American skinhead scene throughout the years, it is difficult to point to any specific year as being the one in which the skinhead band population was at its greatest. To get an accurate picture of skinhead bands, it is easier to break the United States down into regions and discuss some of the main bands from the beginning of skinhead subculture through today.

East Coast

New York

Undoubtedly, the most influential music on the American skinhead scene was New York hardcore. Hardcore was originally just a faster and harder style of punk that started around 1979 to 1980. The style known as NYHC started in the early 1980s and was characterized by "driving machine gun drum beats, fast heavy guitar riffs, and simple repetitive bass lines."[2] Also included in most NYHC was what is now known as "the break down"—a quintessential break in the song that would send the listeners into a full-blown frenzy. The vocals were shouted, and many bands had sing-along choruses to encourage audience participation. Lyrics of songs reflected themes of unity, brotherhood, and social justice. New York hardcore facilitated the use of the term "skinhead" across the United States, and helped define what youths considered "skinhead."

The hub of the early NYHC scene was the apartment of Vinnie Stigma on the Lower East Side. As Stigma describes it, "Back then punk rock was more like new wave with synthesizer, etc. . . . but

Agnostic Front and Father Hank, at CBGB's last hardcore matinee, 2006 (Courtesy of Steven J. Messina).

I musically attacked the guitar and created what is today known as Hardcore." The most popular bands to come from that scene were all created by New York's first crew of skinheads. Members of Agnostic Front (AF), Cro-Mags, Warzone, and Murphy's Law were all friends who lived on the Lower East Side and spent as much time causing a ruckus in the streets as they did creating their revolutionary sound. John Joseph, lead singer of the Cro-Mags, credits their sound to a mix of hardcore and the energy and sound of the Washington, D.C., band, Bad Brains. "Without Bad Brains," he says, "there would be no Cro-Mags." Hardcore matinees at CBGB were the epicenter of skinhead hardcore. Frank, a New York skin, recalls, "Bands like AF and Cro-Mags in '86 pushed everything into gear. You go to a show and everyone was a skinhead—everyone shaved their heads even if they weren't skinheads."

Other notable bands, such as Youth Defense League (YDL), adapted the hardcore sound and mixed it with Oi! YDL was one of the first New York hardcore bands to take a right-wing stance in its music. The group's members described themselves as "being quite off to the right; we're just pro-America."[3] Although some members of YDL certainly flirted with the racist skinhead movement, the band did not publicly embrace this ideology. Other notable New York Oi! bands from the 1980s included Brute Force, American Eagle, and Sick Society. There was no significant White Power music scene in New York, although the NYHC sound was adapted by racist bands in other regions of the United States.

By the late 1980s, many New York skinheads had branched off from the hardcore movement and gravitated toward bands with the more traditional Oi! and Ska sounds. At this time, Ska music enjoyed a third wave of popularity with the emergence of bands such as The Toasters, Scofflaws, and NY Citizens. One of the leading promoters of the third wave of Ska music, Robert "Bucket" Hingley (The Toasters front man), was also the owner of a Ska record label, Moon Records. This label was responsible for issuing a number of compilations that featured both Ska acts and Oi! bands.

One of the first New York bands to adopt the traditional Oi! sound was The Press, which formed in 1984. In 1985, this band recorded and released *Just Another Warning* on a Moon Records compilation, *New York Beat: Hit and Run*. In 1987, The Press recorded

The Templars (Courtesy of Khaki Bedford).

eight songs for the split *Skins 'N' Punks Vol. 5* album, which was released on an English label, Oi! Records. The bands Wretched Ones and Niblick Henbane soon followed. Lead singer of the Wretched Ones, Armen Chaparian, created the well-known Oi label, Headache Records.

In the early 1990s, the New York scene gave birth to a new generation of Oi! bands, such as The Templars, Oxblood, First Strike, Bottom of the Barrel, Battle Cry and Those Unknown from New Jersey.

The spirit of brotherhood embodied by the original hardcore skinhead bands was passed on to this second wave of New York skinhead music. As Phil Templar recalls, "Whenever we had a show, we had Oxblood play with us; whenever they got a show, they said The Templars had to play with them. It was friendship; we were their boys, they were ours."

Today, the hardcore scene that contributed to the birth of American skinheads is still thriving, with bands such as Agnostic Front, Cro-Mags, and Murphy's Law regularly touring all over the world. Even so, the hardcore scene is more distinct from the skinhead subculture and the vast majority of youths who embrace hardcore music do not label themselves skinheads. The Templars continue to enjoy popularity both within and outside the United States, regularly playing large punk festivals all over Europe.

Other Major East Coast Cities

The oldest skinhead band in the United States was Iron Cross from Washington, D.C., whose classic song "Crucified for Our Sins" was later covered by Agnostic Front and became the most well-known American skinhead anthem. Iron Cross's single "Skinhead Glory" was heavily influenced by the British Oi! sound. As one review stated, Sab Grey has vocals reminiscent of the lead singer of the popular British punk band Blitz. Also emerging from the Washington, D.C., scene in the late 1980s was Immoral Discipline, whose music was featured on the *US of Oi* compilation. This group branded its particular kind of music as "Oi-core," representing a fusion of American hardcore and British Oi! Immoral Discipline's most popular song was "Boots and Braces, Stars and Stripes." In a letter to *Maximum Rock n Roll*, lead singer Shawn Garard wrote, "My band has taken a firm stand against [racism] with lyrics condemning race-hating and urging racial unity."[4] Another popular Washington, D.C., band from the late 1990s was Counterattack.

Stormwatch from Delaware was one of the most controversial Oi! bands of the 1990s. Its songs covered topics such as injustice, fighting, and abuse of power. One song was even about the beating of Reginald Denny, a white truck driver attacked during the Los Angeles riots. Stormwatch was a conservative band whose members considered themselves nationalists but not racists.

During the 1980s, a thriving hardcore scene was also found in Boston. The Boston hardcore band Slapshot gained a following among skinheads because of its Oi!-inspired sing-along style. Slapshot's lead singer, Jack "Choke" Kelly also had a popular side band called Stars & Stripes which appeared on the first US of Oi! compilation. Boston also produced the Bruisers, one of America's leading Oi! bands of the late 1980s and early 1990s. In an interview, this band's members stated, "Our lyrics are about family, brotherhood, the crumbling of the Berlin Wall and just plain f*cking sh*t up."[5]

The Bruisers' lead singer, Al Barr, is currently singing for the Dropkick Murphys, which has become the most popular band to emerge from the U.S. skinhead underground. In the punk world, it is well known that Dropkick Murphys started off as an Oi!-inspired band, even covering The Press's "21 Guitar Salute." The Dropkick Murphys' sound has often been characterized as "Celtic punk" because it is a blend of traditional Irish folk music and punk.

Al Barr of the Dropkick Murphys (AP Photo/Keystone/ Peter Klaunzer).

Like New York, Boston also had a flourishing Ska scene at the same time. Bands such as Bim Ska La Bim played shows as early as 1983, and other bands soon followed in its path. The most popular band to emerge from the Boston Ska scene of this era was the Mighty Mighty Bosstones. This band's roots traced to the hardcore scene of the early 1980s, along with a strong influence from the 2Tone style.

The Northeast was also home to a number of other American skinhead bands. In Connecticut, Forced Reality became popular. Pittsburgh spawned the bands Best Defense and Half Life in the 1980s, and is currently home to The Traditionals. Philadelphia was home to White Power skinhead bands such as New Glory, Arresting Officers, and Elite Terror, as well as to the traditional Oi! bands Uprise and Allegiance. The city also produced Bovver 96 in the 1990s.

The South and Southwest

In the 1980s, the South was a hotbed for skinhead music. The biggest bands at that time were the Anti-heroes, Moonstomp, and the Kicker Boys. Atlanta hosted a variety of skinhead music festivals, with the Beer Olympics becoming the most popular annual concert (held from 1996 to 2004). It was not uncommon for more than 400 skinheads to attend these festivals.

Atlanta's first skinhead band was the Anti-Heroes. The group formed in 1984 and soon built up a substantial following with its strong but melodic songs and the biting social commentary of its lyrics. By 1987, the Anti-Heroes were not alone, as other bands appeared on the scene, such as Moonstomp and the Kicker Boys. By 1988, all three of these bands had signed to the British Oi! label, Link Records. All eventually released full LPs and appeared on a variety of Oi! compilations issued by the label.

The end of the 1980s saw the demise of both Moonstomp and the Kicker Boys; in 1992, the Anti-Heroes broke up as well. New bands such as Jack The Lad sprang up in their wake, but the scene began to decline. By 1993, however, things began to rebound with the re-formed Anti-Heroes and new bands such as Adolph and the Piss Artists playing around town and attracting a new group of youths to the skinhead scene.

By 1996, new bands such as Man's Ruin (which featured a skinhead girl singer), Terminus City, and the Breakaways were playing. The Southern scene kept its momentum until about 2000, when skinhead numbers began to decline again. That decline accelerated after the second breakup of the Anti-Heroes in 2001.

Patriot from Chapel Hill, North Carolina, was another major skinhead band of the 1990s, releasing several albums and playing across the United States. The group broke up in 2004, but re-formed in 2007.

The current Southern skinhead scene has kept some momentum going in the new millennium, although Atlanta no longer has the same prominence as it did in the 1980s. Instead, North Carolina has become the most fertile scene, with the founding of bands such as the Antagonizers, Vanguard, ATF, and The Ivy League. Empire Falls was one of the few racist bands to emerge from the North Carolina scene. Florida is home to the bands Los Greencardz (Miami), Lucky Scars

(Tallahassee), and Sick of Society (south Florida), and Texas has The Broadsiders (Dallas) and Roots of Exile (Houston).

The Midwest

When discussing the Midwest, it is difficult to isolate a distinctive sound within the region. While the West Coast launched the "hardcore punk" style and the East Coast brought street-style hardcore into the skinhead scene, there is not the same sort of unifying stylistic element in the Midwest music scene. What the region did become known for was an influx of white supremacist bands from places such as Minneapolis and Oklahoma City. The first racist bands in the United States both hailed from the Midwest—namely, Final Solution from Chicago and White Pride from St. Louis, Missouri. Their music featured a message of racism and hatred toward anyone deemed "nonwhite" and served as the benchmark for other racist bands in the coming decades.

During the 1980s, many non-racist bands also came out of the Midwest region. One such group was Negative Approach, which was formed in Detroit in 1981. By the following year, the band had begun to gain a following with classic songs such as "Can't Tell No One," "Ready to Fight," and "Nothing." Not long after Negative Approach's rise to fame, bassist Pete Zelewski formed the Allied, another influential band. Chicago gave birth to skinhead bands such as Lost Cause in the mid-1980s, and Minneapolis was home to Blind Approach. Additional nonracist skinhead bands from the Midwest include The Service from Milwaukee and Pist'N'Broke from Detroit.

Perhaps one of the more notorious bands to emerge from the Midwest was the Chicago-based band called White American Youth (WAY). This band furthered the negative stereotype of skinheads by later appearing on an HBO special on White Power skinheads. WAY broke up and members formed the band Final Solution in homage to the first White Power band in Chicago, One of the most noteworthy bands of the Midwest White Power scene was Bound for Glory. This Minneapolis-based band, which was formed by Northern Hammerskins leader Ed Wolbank in 1989, quickly became one of the most active touring bands in the genre known as RAC (Rock Against

Communism). Along with Final Solution they were first American White Power bands to play a concert overseas.

Bound for Glory's success was evident by being signed to the same label as Skrewdriver, Rock'O'Rama records. After releasing several albums on the German label, Wolbank and his partner Anthony Pierpont created Panzerfaust Records in 1998 to showcase Bound for Glory as well as other White Power bands.

Currently, there are only a few bands in the Midwest region that embody the principles of today's skinhead scene. Perhaps the most popular is Fear City from Chicago, which plays traditional pub rock featuring chants and lyrics that are very similar to those of their British skinhead counterparts. Pist'N'Broke re-formed in 2009 and recently toured with British Oi! legends The Business.

West Coast

Undisputedly, the first California band that embodied the skinhead look was the Youth Brigade. While they were never skinheads, singer-guitarist Shawn Stern, remembers, "We heard about skinheads from the British bands Madness, Sham 69 and the Angelic Upstarts." Youth Brigade's music was not typical Oi! Rather, like the skinheads in New York, the band members created their own style, which blended California punk and British street rock.

In the 1980s, other bands helped popularize the skinhead hardcore sound. Agression from Oxnard was a favorite of local skinheads and was important to the development of the "Nardcore" scene. Its sound was a mixture of punk and what was called skate rock.

The first California band to try to emulate the Oi! sound was Doug and the Slugs, formed in 1983. As lead singer Doug Kane recalls, "I bought The Last Resort record *Skinhead Anthems* on red vinyl and that was it for me—I started turning everyone on to the music." The violence and meaning of Oi! bands such as The Last Resort, and Sham 69 resonated with Kane's band, and they played local shows in an attempt to create a scene for local skinheads. The short-lived Doug and the Slugs was followed by a few other traditional Oi! bands between 1987 and 1989, including the Bootboys, Headstrong and, Lion's Pride.

Mike Erikson of Pressure Point (Courtesy of oldhcdude).

In Northern California, a revival of the street punk sound was spearheaded by the Swingin' Utters, a band made up of skinheads from Santa Cruz and the band, Reducers SF. The Swingin' Utters have experienced somewhat of a breakthrough success, being featured on the Vans Warped tour and opening for bands such as the Pogues.

The 1990s ushered in a new wave of skinhead bands, including Pressure Point, the Roughnecks, and Tried and True from Northern California, and The Authority, the Toughskins, and Strongarm & the Bullies from the southern end of the state.

California has also been home to a growing White Power music scene. The most well-known band from the 1980s was Youngblood from Orange County. The 1990s and 2000s have seen many racist bands, such as Extreme Hatred, Youngland, and Final War, come and go.

Another distinctive aspect of the skinhead music scene in California was the proliferation of dance clubs whose music catered to the mods and skinheads. In both Northern and Southern California, youths would hold DJ nights as early as 1983. Haunted Studios and later Gino's became the places where skinheads, rudeboys, and mods congregated. Around 1983, local DJs discovered early 1960s Ska and reggae from Jamaica. In turn, DJs from as far away as Santa Cruz

> **Reggae Playlist (Compiled by Gardner "Papa G" Lund)**
>
> 1. "54-46 That's My Number" by The Maytals
> 2. "Skinheads a Bash Dem" by Claudette
> 3. "Wet Dream" by Max Romeo
> 4. "Dollar in the Teeth" by The Upsetters
> 5. "Moon Hop" by Derrick Morgan

expanded the Hollywood-based scene to all parts of California. The impact the California DJs had on the rest of the United States was long lasting. Today most large skinhead scenes have DJs who sponsor soul and reggae dances monthly, including the scenes in New York, Chicago, San Francisco, Los Angeles, and Portland (Oregon).

Also during the 1980s, Los Angeles became home to bands emulating the jumpy Jamaican beats and horns. The most well-known bands to come out of the early L.A. Ska scene were No Doubt, the Untouchables, Let's Go Bowling (actually from Fresno), Hepcat, and Fishbone. By the late 1980s, Northern California bands such as Operation Ivy, Dance Hall Crashers, and the Liquidators also had large followings.

Today, the skinhead scene in California remains the most active on the West Coast. Pressure Point is one of the most popular Oi! bands, while bands such as the Aggrolites and Hepcat keep the Ska/reggae flame alive. Orange County continues to be the largest producer of White Power bands, although most of these bands have abandoned Oi! for the sounds of "hatecore" (racist hardcore) and metal.

While American skinheads listen to local bands, they continue to listen to traditional skinhead music, whether from the 1960s or the

> **Northern Soul Playlist (Compiled by Stormy Rodgers)**
>
> 1. "The Snake" by Al Wilson Soul City
> 2. "Hope We Have" by The Artistics Brunswick
> 3. "Manifesto" by Case of Tyme Legend
> 4. "If That's What You Wanted" by Frankie Beverly and The Butlers Sassy/Rouser
> 5. "This Thing Called Love" by Johnny Wyatt Bronco

Best of Oi! Music (Compiled by Perry Hardy and Tiffini Travis)

1. "Chaos" by 4skins
2. "Oi Oi Oi" by Cockney Rejects
3. "Violence in Our Minds" by Last Resort
4. "Someone's Gonna Die Tonight" by Blitz
5. "Real Enemy" by The Business

1980s. A sampling of the most popular genres of music can be found in the sidebars, which feature lists compiled by DJs.

Notes

1. *Harley's War* video, Magna, 2007.
2. Wood, Robert. "The Indigenous, Nonracist Origins of the American Skinhead Subculture." *Youth and Society* 31, (1999): 131–151, p. 135.
3. Interview in an unidentified fanzine, May 30, 1987.
4. Letter to the editor, *Maximum Rock n Roll*, June 1989.
5. "Interview, Bruisers," *Under Siege Fanzine*, Summer 1992.

CHAPTER FOUR

Skinheads and the Media

The media have had an impact on every youth subculture in the United States. Whether the subculture represents a source of novelty, as has been the case with ravers and skaters, or has been covered with derision, as with hip-hop and punk, every subculture is influenced by the news coverage and the information published about it. This relationship has especially held true for skinheads.

Although skinheads existed for more than a decade in England before they drew U.S. attention, Americans remained largely unaware of their presence. Exposure to skinheads in the United States was limited to news stories on the distinctly British subculture or chance meetings on trips abroad. The first article written about skinheads was published in *The New York Times* in 1969. Basic elements of the subculture were identified in this article, and no references to violence or racism were evident. Three months later, in 1970, *The New York Times* ran an article about the youth phenomenon of skinheads in England. They were presented as "white youths that admire Jamaican Rudys, listen to reggae and whip up riots at soccer games." Their mortal enemies were described as "hippies, homosexuals and Pakis."[1] Another feature story appeared in June 1970 in *Time* magazine. Even though these articles feature

"This well-known image of the racist, violent skinhead has become a familiar tool used in popular films and television shows to evoke fear and hatred within the audiences as an aid to their storyline."

—Sylvia Sievers

skinheads, no indication was ever made about the subculture being copied by American youth.

There was a gap in mentions of skinheads in the mainstream U.S. press from 1971 until the early 1980s, when race riots plagued London. A feature on skinheads appeared in *People* magazine in September 1981.[2] Skinheads were the primary villains in these news reports, which described smashed windows and attacks against Pakistani and black people. In all of these articles, skinheads were presented as a purely British construct, and no reference was made to the subculture having migrated to the shores of the United States.

Most references to American skinheads in the 1980s were limited to alternative publications written by youths, for youths. Skinheads were regularly referred to as "skins" or "skinheads" in alternative punk publications such as *Flipside* and *Maximum Rock n Roll* as early as 1981. The coverage included interviews with bands such as Agnostic Front and Iron Cross, but also focused on violence in the punk scenes attributed to skinheads. In 1983, an editorial appeared in an issue of *Maximum Rock n Roll* about the growing right-wing nature of British skinheads. The article prophetically alluded to the possibility of this transition happening in America as well.

Mainstream media discovered skinheads when the punk scene became large enough to garner attention. At first they were casually lumped together with punks. By 1985, however, stories began appearing that focused solely on the subject of skinheads. Soon the actions of a few defined the image of all skinheads.

Articles with titles such as "Skinheads on the Rampage" and "Chilling Wave of Racism" soon began appearing in the mainstream media. Individual skinheads contributed to this frenzy by perpetrating more crimes against innocent citizens. Reports of assaults against minorities across the United States began appearing by the mid-1980s. In August 1987, a skinhead from San Jose, California, was charged with armed robbery for blocking the path of a black woman until she paid a "n*gger toll." Later that same year, two teenage skinhead brothers, Scott and Dean McKee, were arrested for beating and stabbing a homeless man to death in Tampa, Florida. The reporting of crimes perpetrated by skinheads escalated steadily from 1987 until the early 1990s. During this era, references were made to murders perpetrated by skinheads for reasons ranging from gang initiation to hate crimes. Assaults on minorities and synagogue vandalism were documented by newspapers across the United States, and the result was a wave of hysteria and fear regarding the new threat seemingly posed by skinheads.

The public was struck by the shocking appearance of the subculture and the violence and distaste this new breed of youth seemed to have for society. While punks were seen as nonviolent, often unclean anarchists with leftist leanings, skinheads were perceived as their polar opposites. Most references to skinheads occurred in local newspapers, however; not much coverage of this subculture appeared on television. What the general public failed to realize was that the "crime wave" that was widely publicized through the media was actually perpetrated by a small segment of the total skinhead population. As skinhead researcher Jennifer Bard found, "Most people continue to associate the skinhead movement with neo-Nazi views and violence against Jews, non-whites and homosexuals."[3] She continued, "In reality, there are a variety of different types of skinheads that have no relation to the images portrayed in the popular media." News coverage mainly focused on racist skinheads. As a result of this lopsided coverage, all skinheads were vilified, regardless of their beliefs.

Eventually, skinheads who were not racist began to organize to try to change the stereotype of the subculture, and a few stories were reported that gave a more balanced view. Nevertheless, the coverage of nonracists remained minor, and even in articles about racist skinheads they were often relegated to side notes in media accounts. Carl, the lead singer of The Templars, summed up the view of most nonracist skinheads: "The media portrayal was always BS. They wouldn't have much of a story if they showed a bunch of kids from all races and ethnic backgrounds hanging out having a good time, so they look for the fringe rejects with extreme political views and a tendency for violence. The public wants to be scared and shocked, so that's what the media gives them."

The Rise of the Talk Show Circuit Skins

The broader American populace was first introduced to skinheads on the *Phil Donahue Show*, a popular talk show host of the 1970s and 1980s. The episode, which originally aired in 1986, featured some of the most well-known skinheads in the New York hardcore scene. It marked the first time skinheads were presented on a nationally broadcast television station. Even though this episode represented the first large-scale media exposure of American skinheads, most of the viewing audience did not grasp its significance. Although notable skinheads such as Harley Flanagan, Vinny Stigma, and Jimmy G were featured on the show, the term "skinhead" was mentioned only in passing.

By 1987, afternoon talk shows echoed the growing sensationalism associated with the reports of skinhead violence in the print media; it was not long before competing shows sought out skinhead guests. Racist skinheads garnered the most media attention. Television shows such as those hosted by Phil Donahue and Morton Downey, Jr., broadcast several episodes featuring racists between 1987 and 1988. The most infamous talk show appearance occurred on February 4, 1988, on the *Oprah Winfrey Show*. The audience featured a mix of nonracist skinheads, while the stage was filled with racist skinheads and non-skinhead members of White Aryan Resistance (WAR).

Later that year, in October, the scene was repeated on the talk show *Geraldo*. The tension on the stage boiled over when civil rights activist Roy Innis moved toward a Nazi skinhead, Bob Heick. During the ensuing melee, Geraldo suffered a broken nose and many of the guests were ejected from the show.

Memorable televised scenes of snarling racists and chair-flinging brawls meant a leap in the amount of coverage of skinheads in the mainstream media. It also increased the number of youths attracted to the subculture. A by-product of the media coverage of skinheads was a growth in the number of youths becoming skinheads. One researcher noted that 97 percent of the skinheads she surveyed in 2003 found out about the subculture by seeing them on television, movies, or news programs, or by hearing about them through friends, parents, or others.[4] The founder of the White Aryan Resistance, Tom Metzger said, "After *Oprah* and *Geraldo*, our recruiting went up at least 100 percent."[5]

White supremacists had an advantage in getting their word out to the masses, largely due to the training they had from established organizations such as White Aryan Resistance and Aryan Nations. Tom Metzger created *WAR* magazine, specifically targeting youths. He also used closed-circuit television as a platform for producing the series *Race and Reason*. Recognizing the value of television, Metzger doubled his production output between 1985 and 1986, with his show being syndicated in a number of cities across the United States.

In addition to promoting their own publications, WAR and other racist skinhead groups regularly reached out to the media in an effort to spread the word. They appeared on local television shows and even news channels such as CNN. Whereas talk shows regularly invited members from groups such as NAACP and the Southern Poverty Law Center to participate in their broadcasts, antiracist skinheads were often omitted from the dialogue. The result of the narrow media spotlight meant that racist organizations dominated the public's perception of skinhead, which further pigeon-holed the subculture. Suddenly the scourge of the skinhead was upon America, it was felt, and some of the more vocal groups took advantage of the hysteria.

After the media became aware of the existence of skinheads in the United States, watchdog groups such as the Anti-Defamation League (ADL) and even the Federal Bureau of Investigation (FBI) began to take notice and monitor groups in earnest. Information was collected and promulgated by the media on a regular basis. The most popular reports included the ADL Special Report, *Shaved for Battle*, published in 1987 and *Young and Violent: The Growing Menace of America's Neo-Nazi Skinheads*, published in 1988. Collectively, the ADL and the FBI account for the majority of statistics published about skinheads by news media outlets.

Many traditional skinheads identify this intense media scrutiny as the beginning of the demise of the skinhead scene. Soon, everyone called themselves skinheads, and the lunatic fringe increasingly garnered the spotlight, further destroying what had been a counterculture that had existed without the outside watching. Unfortunately, the legacy of the mainstream media portrayal of skinheads lives on even today. If the average American is asked what a skinhead is, he or she will undoubtedly define such a person as white, racist, and violent.

Skinheads for Skinheads: Vanity Publishing and the Cult

For the youths involved in the skinhead subculture, their primary source of information was other skinheads. In the early days, the most prominent publications focusing on the subculture came from the United Kingdom. Some of the more popular books that followed in the next 20 years included *Skins* by Gavin Watson, *Skinhead Nation* by George Marshall, and later the reprinted editions of the Richard Allen Skinhead pulp fiction series featuring the character Joe Hawkins.

While many U.K. titles were distributed in the United States, two titles in particular had a profound impact on the American skinhead

Skinhead *by Nick Knight was one of the first books about skinheads (Chris Schaefer).*

scene. The first was *Skinhead* by Nick Knight. It was primarily a picture book of the second wave of British skinheads from the late 1970s and early 1980s. In addition to showing pictures of skinheads, it included a graphical look at skinhead fashion from the first wave in 1969 to the early 1980s. It featured photos of London skinheads of the early 1980s, drawings of 1960s and 1970s skinhead and suedehead dress styles, and some text about the original reggae skinhead scene. American skinhead crews such as Toehead Army from Southern California fashioned themselves after the book, and for some it was the gateway to the original style and behaviors of the subcultures in England.

The second title was *Spirit of '69: A Skinhead Bible*. Written by George Marshall, a skinhead from Glasgow, Scotland, in 1991, it was a compilation of pictures and newspaper clippings, and an impartial retelling of the history of skinheads. It focused primarily on British skinheads, but contained images of skinheads from all over the world. It also included a section on left- and right-wing politics. Some researchers believe the publication of this book was at least partly responsible for the rise of the traditional skinheads across the United States. *Spirit of '69* gave skinheads a chance to be something other than a Nazi skinhead. Twenty years after it was originally published, Marshall's book has become extremely rare, selling for as much as $350 on websites such as eBay.

As the subculture has matured in the United States and technology has facilitated self-publishing, more and more vanity books have been published on the topic of skinheads. Self-published titles have been released all over Europe and the United States, featuring pictures of skinheads around the world. Some of these titles are printed in the hundreds of copies, whereas others are available only in limited runs. All are of varying quality, but each offers a snapshot of the current skinhead scene and a glimpse at some of the trends that are present in different regions.

Fanzines and Internet Sites

As an underground subculture, skinheads have always had to rely on alternative means to get their music and messages out to the world. Before the Internet became widely available, the primary means of communication was the printed word. The primary sources of information about skinheads were fanzines—that is, small-run magazines usually produced and distributed by individual punks and skinheads. The longevity of a fanzine depended on the dedication of the individual putting it out. Life spans might range from 2 issues to 20 issues. Skinheads had pen-pals in different cities and sometimes in different countries, and letters were exchanged detailing what was happening in different places. Fanzines typically included music reviews, fanzine reviews, concert reviews, scene reports, and other skinhead-related information. For many skinheads, such publications were the only way to get news about the subculture. In the 1980s and 1990s, fanzines (or 'zines as they are called) served as a vital communication link that bound the scene together.

Fanzines first became prominent media tools after punk broke in England in the late 1970s—punk was one of the first youth subcultures that did not rely on the mainstream press to disseminate its message. Early American punk 'zines such as *Slash* and *Flipside* played a similar role in the United States.

With the rise of the Oi! music scene in the early 1980s, the first skinhead fanzines appeared. Fanzines were the voice of skinhead culture during the 1980s and 1990s. International fanzines such as *Boots and Braces*, *Skins*, *Skinhead Times*, and *Backs Against the Wall* began to find their way to America, and some U.S. skinheads began to start up fanzines of their own.

American Skinhead Fanzines

The first of these publications was *Skinflint*, which was published by Sab Grey of the band Iron Cross. Other skinhead fanzines appeared throughout the 1980s as the skinhead population grew. *Running Riot*, *Back with a Bang*, *Real Threat*, *Bulldog Breed*, and hundreds of others appeared, although some lasted for only a short period of time. Many of these publications catered to the White Power scene. *Dixie Rose* from the Southwest and Detroit's *Final War* and *Hail Victory* were popular 'zines. At the same time, however, both traditional and nonpolitical fanzines flourished as well.

Perhaps the most important antiracist 'zine was *Boots-N-Booze*, which was published by a group of skinheads in Santa Cruz, California. Even though only 12 issues were ultimately published, this fanzine

---

Skinhead Writers: Skinheads have turned to publishing novels, autobiographies, and even comic books detailing their lives as skinheads.

Sab Grey: *Skinhead Army.*
Pete Kalafatis: *A Rebel Life: Murder by the Rich*
Chris Picciolini: *Romantic Violence: Memoirs of an American Skinhead*
TJ Leyden: *Skinhead Confessions*
Greg Narvas: *I Was a Teenage Filipino Skinhead*

---

helped contribute to the revival of the traditional skinhead subculture across the United States.

Another relevant 'zine from the late 1980s was *American Skinhead,* which was put together by a group of skinheads from Southern California. *American Skinhead* focused more on the Oi! music scene than did *Boots-N-Booze,* but was just as antiracist in its approach.

As the 1980s came to an end, many of the original American skinzines ceased publication, while others started up to fill the void. Perhaps the biggest of this new breed was *Boot Party* out of Chicago. Six issues of this fanzine appeared between 1989 and 1992, and the circulation increased to 700 copies for each of the last two issues, including readers in Japan and several European countries as well as all over the United States.

Other fanzines were produced by skinheads all over the United States, including *Carry No Banners* (Florida/Illinois), *A Way of Life* (Hawaii), *Under Siege* (Indiana), *No Escape* (New York), and *United Front* (North Carolina). Each fanzine played a vital role in the development of the American skinhead scene in the 1990s.

With the arrival of the Internet, new forms of communication were established. As a consequence, the print fanzine has almost completely died out, being replaced by blogs, Internet portals, and social networking sites.

The Rise of the Internet

One of the by-products of the flourishing fanzine publications was the spread of the skinhead subculture. Not only did they publicize

Skinheads.net logo (Chris Nutter).

skinhead music, but some fanzines would also discuss other topics specific to the culture, including dress and values. Since its inception, The internet has become a significant tool in maintaining the popularity of the skinhead subculture. Just as the print fanzines of the 1980s and 1990s allowed skinheads to find other skinheads, so the Internet exponentially increased the contact between skinheads, both nationally and internationally.

As connectivity spread across the United States, websites such as Skinhead FAQ, Bottom of the Barrel, and Real Skinheads.net became the primary source of online news and information about this subculture. Today, the most popular American skinhead Internet site is Skinheads.net, which is run by veteran Atlanta skinhead Chris Nutter. Nutter describes the early days of his website:

> Circa 1997, computers were getting big, and I thought I should learn a little about them. Then I decided I wanted a web page. I tried to create something that was for skinheads by skinheads, and it basically wound up being Skinheads.net. It's been going ever since.

In its current incarnation, Skinheads.net is a forum where people can come and talk about whatever they feel like talking about. Nutter has kept the site completely nonpolitical. He says, "I personally attempt to discourage any racists from being on the site. We do have some, but we also have some communists, too. But the vast majority [of users] are just skinheads in general who have no political leanings whatever." Currently, Skinheads.net is the largest skinhead website, with an estimated 8,000 registered users worldwide, of whom 600 to 700 are regularly active on its message boards.

Blood and Honour website (AP PHOTO/screenshot).

The Internet has made being a skinhead a lot easier, offering instant access to clothes, music, and news. Social networking sites such as Facebook and music sites like LastFM and Reverbnation have become extremely important to the skinhead scene across the world. Just about every band has a profile page where it posts up-to-the-minute news on upcoming gigs, tours, CD and DVD releases, and other information. Likewise sites like eBay enable international distribution of skinhead related items. Using these sites, skinheads can network with fellow skinheads the world over, and have access to music and clothing items that skinheads in the 1980s and 1990s could only have dreamed of. This instant access to information has led to a sustained interest in the subculture by newer generations of youths.

As early as 1995, racist groups embraced the Internet as a means of spreading their message of hate. Because free speech is one of the key precepts on which the Internet was founded, extremist groups were quick to recognize its value in their cause. One article noted, "You can post messages on electronic bulletin boards where potentially millions of people can read your information. You can debate anti-racists or just post racialist ideology and information."[6] Not only do most major racist organizations have websites and domain name servers (DNS), but they have also created an elaborate network for connecting members. Like the other sites mentioned, the racist websites are used to distribute music, literature, and merchandise. In fact, the success of some later White Power organizations such as the Hammerskins was due almost entirely to electronic communication. As a former Western Hammerskin noted, "I had a lot of interaction with skinheads throughout the entire world. With the Internet it was a lot easier to push information out and to make connections between our chapter members."

Skinheads in Film

Like the original books about the skinhead subculture, movies about skinheads were primarily U.K. productions. The first film distributed in the United States featuring skinheads was the film *Dance Craze* in 1982. This documentary about the 2Tone movement featured bands that had skinhead members, such as Madness.

The first American film that prominently featured a skinhead character was *Suburbia* (1983), directed by Penelope Spheeris. The film featured a real skinhead, Timothy O'Brien, whose name in the film was Skinner. In addition to having a realistic portrayal of the typical skinhead in the punk scene, *Suburbia* featured references to

---

Skinheads on the Small Screen: From 1988 until today, skinheads have been featured on television drama and documentaries. These are just a few of the more popular shows.

De Grassi Junior High (1988 to 1991)
21 Jump Street (1990)
HBO: *Skinheads USA: Soldiers of the Race War* (1993)
Hate Rock: An MTV News Special Report (1993)
Law and Order (1995)
Discovery Channel: *Gang Nation* (2006)
National Geographic: *Inside American Skinheads* (2007)
History Channel: *Gangland* (2007; 2009)

skinhead bands and music in the graffiti that appears on the walls of the fictional crash pad, TR house.

The skinhead look was also present in the film *Another State of Mind* (1984), which chronicles a 1982 tour of the bands Youth Brigade and Social Distortion. While the majority of youths were not skinheads by definition, they still managed to project the look to a large populace of American kids. This film, as well as *Suburbia*, was seen on the national cable channel USA as part of its popular late-night film series, *Night Flight*.

When skinheads gained the interest of the media, a series of dramatic films were produced that further perpetuated the stereotype of racist skinheads, as in the campy *Skinheads: The Second Coming of Hate* (1989) and John Singleton's *Higher Learning* (1995). While a few movies focused completely on skinhead characters, such as *Made in Britain* (1983), *Romper Stomper* (1992), *The Believer* (2001), and *16 Years of Alcohol* (2004), none had more of an impact on skinheads in the United States than the film *American History X*. Released in 1998, it starred Ed Norton and Edward Furlong. The film was a phenomenal financial success and promoted the racist skinhead image to a new generation of American youths.

The last fictional film to be produced was probably the most accurate portrayal of skinheads in the United Kingdom called *This is England* (2006). Written and directed by Shane Meadows, it is based on his own experience as a youth in 1980s England. Similar to George Marshall's book *Spirit of '69*, this film examined both racist and nonracist skinhead life and provided the most realistic and balanced portrayal of the skinhead subculture to date.

Notes

1. Nik Cohn, "Pop: England's New Teen Style Is Violence," *New York Times* (March 29, 1970), 99.
2. Fred Hauptfuhrer and Terry Smith, "With Ready Fists and Rage, Britain's Skinheads Alarm an Already Troubled Country," *People* 16 (September 1981), 53–54.
3. Jennifer Lynn Bard, *An Exploratory Analysis of Youth in Skinhead Groups* (M.A. thesis, Simon Fraser University, Canada, 1999), 25.

4. Sylvia Jane Sievers, *American Skinheads: An Investigation into the Acquisition of a Deviant Identity* (Ph.D. dissertation, State University of New York at Stony Brook, 2003).

5. Pete George Simi, *Rage in the City of Angels: The Historical Development of the Skinhead Subculture in Los Angeles* (Ph.D. dissertation, University of Nevada, Las Vegas, 2003), 106.

6. Tony McAleer, "Plug Into the Freedom of the Internet," *Resistance Magazine* (1995), 13.

| # Race and Nation: The Politicization of American Skinheads

While it is well documented that nonracist skinheads largely outnumbered racist rivals in many cities, media coverage often overlooked the war raging in the streets between the two groups, giving the impression that all skinheads were white supremacists. In reality, the politicization of the skinhead subculture is more complex.

Skinheads have always had political awareness in the subculture, whether it be identifying with a particular social class or the innate nationalistic stance echoed in the lyrics of skinhead music. To a certain extent, skinhead life was a reaction to the anarchist slant of many of the punk bands from the 1980s. All skinheads adopted similar values regarding family, class, and nation. Being patriotic was a staple of the skinhead lifestyle, regardless of political or ethnic identification. Skinheads adorned their flight jackets with American flags, and skinhead bands wrote lyrics that emulated the nationalistic lyrics of their British counterparts. Conservatism was customary in the scene even among the nonpolitical adherents, and a disdain for "hippies" and "dirty punks" was embraced by many.

As the National Front gained a stronghold in the British skinhead scene in the early 1980s, right-wing music filtered into the United States and was consumed by American skinheads. One of the most

Racist rally in Pulaski, Tennessee, 1989 (AP Photo/Mark Humphrey).

popular of these bands, Skrewdriver, was actively endorsing the politics of the National Front through its racist lyrics in songs like *White Power* and *Hail the New Dawn*. By 1985, the first clusters of racists were present in cities such as Chicago and San Francisco. While there were always undercurrents of racism in the American skinhead scene, an explosion of skinheads identifying themselves with White Pride or White Power occurred by 1987. As Dannyboy, a skinhead from San Francisco described it, fences were erected between groups of skinheads and lines were drawn: "I tried to stay friends with both racist and non-racist friends but after awhile it became clear you had to choose one side or the other. That's when I moved toward the traditional side of skinhead to distance myself from the Nazis."

Other skinheads decided to move in the opposite direction and embraced racist ideology. When asked why he started to associate with

> "There is definitely a war going on within a subculture of society, and 99 percent of us aren't aware that it's happening except for those moments when it spills out and a Jew or a black is assaulted."
> —Chip Berlet, Political Research Associates

White Power skinheads rather than the nonpolitical side, one skinhead had this to offer: "I was taken advantage of and manipulated and thought the 'cool guys' side was the White Power side." He continued, "I was never raised to hate anybody . . . and they managed to blame my problems on the fact that I was persecuted for being white." Another skinhead who was an avowed racist for more than 10 years said, "I was a racist skinhead and I had no one to blame but myself. It was my choice and my decision and it's something I have to live with."

Starting in 1987, many skinhead crews splintered, or purged some of their members, based on race-based principles. It was not uncommon for skinheads to be kicked out of crews because of their beliefs. Some crews did not allow racists, whereas others kicked out members of color. The result was a polarization of the scene.

For many skinheads who identified themselves as Nazis or White Power advocates, dabbling with racism was a passing phase. As one skinhead explains, "We claimed to be right wing because it was a way of offending the system." It was common to hear youths refer to themselves as standing for "White Pride" rather than being racist or to accept some races and reject others. As one California skinhead complained, "The thing that bugs me in this scene is that white people can't be proud of their race because it's politically incorrect. You can say 'Brown Pride' but the second you say 'White Pride' you are a racist." Some skinheads would drift back and forth between the two sides of the scene and were commonly referred to as "fencewalkers." While this stratification was occurring within the scene, the rest of America was largely unaware that skinheads existed. This situation changed, however, when racist skinheads called attention to themselves and caught the eye of the media.

In the mid-1980s, American record stores began to carry the music of Skrewdriver and other English bands who operated under the White Power banner. While listening to racist music did not make youths become racist, it served as an effective method for forging bonds between independent clusters of racist skinheads. In addition to the hard, fast, aggressive sound of this music, the lyrics were anti-Semitic and filled with references to racist ideology. American racist music distributor George Burdi attributed 95 percent of the popularity of the youth hate movement worldwide to White Power music.

The growth of grassroots White Power music enabled racists to organize large concerts across the United States. Such events provided a method of gathering geographically dispersed groups and enticing curious youth for recruiting. One of the most notorious series of gatherings was the Aryan Fest, first held in Missouri in1988. Other Aryan Fests were held in various parts of the United States as well, including Oklahoma, Indiana, California, and Oregon. At an Aryan Fest in 1992, the British White Power band No Remorse was covertly flown into the country to perform. Today, underground White Power shows continue to occur; they are advertised via word of mouth and racist websites. The underground status of these shows is due to the possibility of public protest or venues canceling the events once they realize the controversial nature of the shows. As a result, many festivals are held on private property and in remote locations.

In addition to music, their propensity for intimidation and violence helped to increase the notoriety of racist skinheads. Groups routinely passed out literature, organized marches, and attacked individuals based on race or sexual orientation. These actions gave racist skinheads visibility outside the punk and skinhead scenes and accounted for the majority of news stories about skinheads in the late 1980s. Skinheads who did not subscribe to the racist ideology felt as if their lifestyle had been stolen.

In 1989, in response to the sudden threat posed by racist skinheads, the U.S. Department of Justice established a skinhead taskforce within its civil rights division. Its actions included a crackdown on many of the most prominent and active white supremacist groups, which in turn contributed to their demise in the mid-1990s. Methods used by law enforcement included raiding houses, issuing "do not associate" clauses, and confiscating racist paraphernalia. Officers would go through personal address books, copy phone numbers, and take personal papers. In California, which was one of the most active areas of racist gangs, arrest rates of skinheads for violence-related crimes nearly doubled in Los Angeles County. In Orange County, they increased by 33 percent.

The rise of the White Power forces in the skinhead scene led to a counterattack by, and the growth of, a fervent antiracist skinhead movement. The multicultural aspect of skinheads was all but dismissed by mainstream media. As one observer noted, "It was like no one knew there were two kinds of skinheads except for us kids and so it was up to us to fight it out." In an effort to raise awareness of the existence of nonracist skinheads, groups such as Anti-Racist Action (ARA) and Skinheads Against Racial Prejudice (SHARP) were born. While there had always been skinhead crews who openly warred with racist crews in their cities, ARA and SHARP were the first to take an organized stance against racism.

Birth of a Nation

WAR Skins became one of the most prominent racist organizations in the skinhead scene in the late 1980s. The group was an offshoot of White Aryan Resistance, a group founded by a former Ku Klux Klan member, Tom Metzger. Metzger is credited with being the first mainstream white supremacist to embrace skinheads and bring them into his organization. He said of his involvement with skinheads, "I give them guidance on the law to stay out of trouble, and I give them our ideology. They have their own subculture, and tampering with it would destroy it." The training that Metzger provided to skinheads included setting up WAR phone lines in local cities and post office boxes for correspondence with other racist groups.

WAR Skins holds the distinction of being one of the first skinhead crews to organize based on beliefs rather than geographic location. Whereas CASH was limited to the Chicago, WAR manifested itself all over California. The approach Metzger took when encouraging this new branch of his organization was described as "leaderless resistance." The groups were *guided* by the elder Metzger, rather than *controlled*. Metzger encouraged members of the WAR Skins group to control their own direction by determining chapter rules and managing membership. As one skinhead remembers, the extent of Metzger's

> "WAR wears no uniform, carries no membership card, and takes no secret oath. WAR doesn't' require you to march around a muddy street. WAR works the modern way with thousands of friends doing their part behind the scenes with the system serving their race."
> —WAR flyer

involvement was minimal: "People would seek out Metzger through the Aryan Youth Movement and WAR, and he put us in contact with the groups that contacted him." This form of dispersed leadership appealed to young skinheads, as it gave WAR Skins the appearance of being a movement solely ran by other skinheads.

The first chapter of WAR Skins was founded in Orange County, California, in 1987. The first members included some of the most vocal racist skinheads from that era: TJ Lydon, Dave Mazella, and Marty Cox. Hate crimes in Orange County spiked to an all-time high during the tenure of the WAR Skins, although it is unclear how many of these attacks and vandalism can be attributed to members of the group and how many were the result of copycats in and around Orange County.

In 1988, WAR Skins was documented by law enforcement as including approximately 50 members. This relatively small number did not reflect the much larger size of the nonracist population of skinheads in the Los Angeles area. In fact, this disparity between racist and nonracist skinheads kept WAR Skins from becoming a formidable force in the group's immediate scene. Members' activities were limited to the suburbs and outlying areas where other racist gangs were active. Specifically, WAR Skins was loosely affiliated with the Order Skins in West Covina and Reich Skins in the San Fernando Valley.

In his capacity as a leader of the Southern California chapter of WAR Skins, Dave Mazzella was instrumental in connecting to active racists in the north. He introduced Bob Heick from American Front to Tom Metzger, and set the plan in motion for expanding WAR Skins to Northern California.

The Northern California Chapter of WAR Skins was founded in 1988. Although it was based in the Salinas and Hollister areas, this group recruited across Silicon Valley. Very quickly, the core group grew to approximately 17 members. To ensure that they allowed in men worthy of being members of WAR, nominees for membership had to await the results of a formal vote: "We didn't trust anybody and rejected a lot of people that tried to join." As a founding member, Chuck, recalled, "While there were as many as 20 members, there were at least 60 other youths that hung around with the crew. As a consequence, a lot of stuff was attributed to the WAR Skins even if it wasn't actual members committing criminal acts."

The last chapter of WAR Skins in California was based in San Diego. This chapter was made up of former members of the Bomber Boys gang. The Bomber Boys were initially a crew that was not defined by racist beliefs, and its leaders Bobby and Joe Matiljan were biracial (their mother was black and their father white). Ironically, it was Joe Matiljan who first contacted Tom Metzger about becoming involved with WAR. Initially Metzger welcomed the interest, but once it was revealed that Joe was of mixed race, Metzger no longer communicated with him. By 1987, the racist members had left the Bomber Boys and renamed their group WAR Skins.

At the height of its popularity, WAR Skins had chapters in Los Angeles, Orange County, Redwood City, Riverside, Salinas, San Diego, San Jose, and Turlock. By 1988, law enforcement reported that there were nearly 200 WAR Skins members in the Los Angeles/ Orange County area. Members of the organization regularly fraternized with other racist groups across the United States. One of their most notorious alliances was with a Portland skinhead gang called East Side White Pride (ESWP). ESWP members were convicted of murdering an Ethiopian immigrant named Mulugeta Seraw in November 1988. Not only did the murder trial bring WAR to the forefront of the White Power movement, but it also marked the end of Metzger's official involvement with WAR Skins.

As early as 1989, Metzger had realized that his experiment with decentralized organization of skinheads was quickly getting out of control. Worse still, the reckless actions of the youth were being attributed to his organization and he sensed there would be trouble. Unfortunately for Metzger, even though he asked some chapters to quietly disassociate with WAR after the murder in Portland, he did not act quickly enough to avoid being sued in civil court in 1990 for the murder of Mulugeta Seraw. The judgment against him forced Metzger and his organization to declare bankruptcy.

American Front

Once the power of WAR Skins declined in Northern California, American Front grew in prominence. In 1988, former members of the northern chapter of WAR gravitated to American Front, and the latter group's numbers swelled. American Front was active from 1986 until 1991, with the height of its popularity occurring in the 1988–1990 period. Led by Bob Heick, the group terrorized people in the Haight-Ashbury district and organized marches in San Francisco. The White Workers Day march in 1988 along Haight Street went unopposed. By the second year counter-protests were organized via telephone trees. One member of American Front recalls, "Nothing was announced ahead of time and we marched on city hall but without protesters." In 1990, the group planned another march, only this time at Union Square and the plans were announced a month in advance. Opposition had time to mobilize and the result was 13 members versus an estimated 250 protesters. Trashcans were thrown at skinheads with some members being punched by the crowd. Looking back on the event, a member says, "you got to admit it takes balls to march when you are outnumbered like that." The American Front had to be escorted from the site of the march by the police to avoid serious injury. Two members were hospitalized and the other members were taken to jail. The riot was covered by local and national media.

The charismatic nature of Bob Heick, the leader of the group, enabled American Front to garner media attention. Heick soon became one of the most recognized faces of the racist movement. In addition to making several television appearances, he was interviewed by *Rolling Stone* magazine in 1988 and a teen girls' magazine, *Sassy*, in 1989. In March 1989, Heick attempted to organize one of the earliest musical gatherings featuring white supremacist bands. Later, the event was jokingly dubbed the "Aryan Wood-Flop," after the group's permit was denied due to a public outcry. Although bands flew to California, no actual festival occurred. A side effect of the non-event was the gathering of members from groups such as the Confederate Hammerskins from Dallas and WAR Skins from Southern California.

When the group's power was at its height, chapters of American Front sprouted up in other California cities, including Bakersfield, Rocklin, San Francisco, and West Covina. The organization had affiliate chapters in New Jersey as well as Florida. An attempt to maintain the San Francisco chapter was orchestrated by Paul Parrazzo, who was named the National Chairman shortly after Heick's departure. His efforts were short-lived, and the last of the original American

Front members moved away or ceased their involvement in the organization.

In 2002, American Front was revived in Sacramento, California, by former Florida chapter head David Lynch. Lynch was murdered in March 2011 at his home in Citrus Heights, California.

Hammerskins

One of the most notorious white supremacist groups to emerge during the 1980s was the Dallas crew, known as the Confederate Hammerskins (CHS). It was started by Sean "Hellbent" Tarrant, his then-girlfriend Liz Sherry, and other local skinheads. Initially, Tarrant was a nonpolitical skinhead with a reputation for being violent in the Dallas scene. As one of his early skinhead friends recalled, "We used to hug each other like brothers but when he got out of jail, Hellbent was different . . . I asked him what he was up to and he replied, 'I am fighting for my race,' and that was the end of our friendship."

The idea to start CHS was developed after a few Dallas skinheads spent six months in Chicago with CASH. As one founding member remembers, "We got into street fights with SHOC (Skinheads of Chicago) and the RCP (Revolutionary Communist Party) and after we got back we decided to form into CHS." It didn't take long for CHS to rise to prominence owing to its active pursuit of racial violence. As was the case with other racist groups across the nation, CHS members dominated the local punk shows and beat up anyone who protested their racist stance. Like CASH, they used intimidation of minorities to establish themselves as a menace to the city of Dallas. Unfortunately for CHS, their actions also attracted the attention of law enforcement. In September 1989, group members Sean Tarrant, Jon Jordan, Michael Lawrence, Christopher Greer, and Daniel Wood were arrested for a series of crimes. The Confederate Hammerskins have the distinction of being the first skinheads to be prosecuted by the federal government for violating the civil rights of others.

The first charge stemmed from CHS's actions in denying minorities the ability to use a public park. According to court records, Hammerskins went to the Robert E. Lee Park, "patrolled" in small groups, and chased, beat, and assaulted any nonwhites whom they found there. As a result of these attacks, a number of victims testified that they were afraid to use the park. The Hammerskins were also convicted for painting swastikas, anti-Semitic slogans, and graffiti on the walls of the Jewish Community Center and temple, and for using firearms during the commission of these crimes when they shot out the windows.

During the course of the trial, a number of CHS turned informants and the leadership of the gang was given sentences that ranged from five to nine years. Tarrant was sentenced to nine years. "I can't help but feel that we are our worst enemies at times," Liz Sherry reflected later. "Much of our growth, I believe, was due to the heavy publicity in the beginning."

What remained of CHS was disorganized, and the group became a less influential force in the Dallas scene. Their activities were isolated to random acts of violence—but when CHS members acted, the results usually had deadly consequences. One of the more disturbing crimes attributed to the group was the 1991 murder of an African American teen by three 16-year-old Hammerskins in Arlington, Texas.

By this time, CHS members had begun to refer to themselves as Hammerskins. Other chapters of the gang were also formed across the United States, including the Northern Hammerskins, Eastern Hammerskins, and Western Hammerskins. In 1994, "Hammerskin Nation" solidified itself by officially eliminating regional chapters, although many of the regional groups still referred to themselves by their geographic designation. Today there are active Hammerskin chapters in continental Europe and the United Kingdom. The Hammerskins have the distinction of being the most widespread white supremacist skinhead group in the United States.

At the same time that the White Power groups coalesced, a number of skinheads across the United States organized to fight against them. The most prominent of these crews were ARA and SHARP.

The Syndicate

The Anti-Racist Action (ARA) group was born out of the recognition that one antiracist crew was not sufficient to battle the growing number of rival white supremacist crews. In Uptown South Minneapolis,

> "Neo-Nazi Skinheads—sometimes referred to as boneheads—are somewhat despised by other skinheads for co-opting the skinhead image and attaching it to a system of values which contradicts the marriage of different racial and cultural styles on which the true skinhead subculture is based."
>
> —Researcher Jennifer Bard

the Nazi problem had started to pose a real threat to nonracist skinheads. A local crew called the Baldies found themselves deeply embroiled in an all-out war with the Nazi group White Knights in the streets of downtown Minneapolis. Sometimes the battles were one-on-one, but mostly mob rule was the norm. In early 1986, the Baldies decided they wanted to organize and get more people motivated to fight against racists—that is, to move from spontaneous action to organizing beyond geographic lines. One member of the Baldies, Kieran, read scene letters from *Maximum Rock n Roll* and noticed other skinhead crews were having the same issues in their towns. After corresponding with numerous groups, in 1989 the Baldies decided to hold a regional meeting of skinheads from Chicago, Milwaukee, Cincinnati, St. Paul, and Minneapolis. 70 and 80 people gathered in a public library meeting room. During this meeting, an alliance created what was later called Anti-Racist Action or the Syndicate.

Some chapters included people who were not skinheads; others, such as the Chicago chapter, were skinhead-only organizations. ARA chapters were instrumental in educating nonracist skinheads on how to organize and work with the community. Their efforts were twofold. First, they sought to raise awareness that real skinheads were not racist and identified with a pro-working-class, multicultural heritage. Second, they engaged in physical confrontation of racists. In cities such as Chicago, their activism reached beyond the efforts of any typical skinhead crew. They regularly met with local business owners and nonprofit groups to find funding for the scene and events. At shows, members of the ARA set up tables for flyers and various local causes. When the Internet became popular, chapters were taught how to create websites.

One of the other actions that the ARA handled was sending organizers around the United States to help mobilize antiracist groups in cities with large White Power populations. Marty Williams, a member of the Chicago chapter remembers, "Many of us decided to travel to other cities with the intent of building a network of shared experiences, organizational strategy, and camaraderie amongst like-minded individuals." As the Nazi problem in Portland escalated, ARA sent representatives to create an antiracist skinhead crew in the Oregon city. By 1992, Williams acknowledges, "ARA had evolved from a primarily skinhead-based crew to a national organization in many cities attracting students, workers, anarchist punks, and older, more established leftist activists."

By 1998, ARA had an estimated 2,000 punk and skinhead members, with chapters in 11 U.S. states, Germany, and Colombia. While chapters of ARA are still sprinkled across the United States, many of the original members of ARA have since moved on to other subcultures or outgrown the skinhead lifestyle altogether. Some of the hardcore members of the original Midwest chapters drifted toward more extreme politics, embracing the revolutionary rhetoric of social movements such as that espoused by the Black Panthers.

SHARP

SHARP was born in New York in 1987 in response to the rise of white supremacist elements, whose views were reported more widely in the media. An original member recounted, "SHARP started in NYC from a small crew of personal friends. They went to shows handing out flyers and recruiting members, making a show of force if nothing else, which meant a great deal in the beginning when people were fast to talk about anti-racism but slow to actually act on it." He continued, "Marcus (Pacheco) came up with the concept, designed a logo, had it made into patches, organized meetings and the activities."

By 1988, the small crew had evolved into a group with 30 to 40 members. Its primary purpose was to educate the general public

---

"True skinheads have no affiliation with fascism and fascist organizations. Don't believe the Hype!"

—SHARP flyer

that "being a skinhead is a style and a cultural choice, not a political one." Original members created SHARP for one specific reason: to fight fascists. As an original member, Andre Schlesinger, wrote on his website, "In the beginning SHARP wasn't necessarily political although SHARP's mission would dictate that it would eventually need to become politically conscious." SHARP, like the Baldies, took a militant stance against racist skinheads and often partnered with antiracist crews in other cities.

In an effort to organize the existing chapters, the first national SHARP Conference was organized in Cincinnati. Soon chapters had sprung up across the United States, including in Portland, Houston, and Los Angeles. Some chapters were robust and active, whereas others did not last for more than a year.

To battle against racist skinheads, SHARP (like ARA) had no problem fighting violence with violence. Following the murder of Mulugeta Seraw, it was alleged that members of the Portland chapter of SHARP dragged two females from a convenience store and beat them with a hammer. Scotti from the New York chapter remembers being permanently banned from a punk clothing store for fighting in the store aisles with local Nazis.

In 1989, Roddy Moreno, lead singer for the British skinhead band The Oppressed, learned of the organization. He started the first SHARP chapter in the United Kingdom; other chapters quickly sprouted up all over Europe.

While official SHARP chapters had largely died out in the United States by 1995, some skinheads continue to lay claim to this designation. Schlesinger sums up the current state of the organization in this way:

> As it is today SHARP is unorganized. It lacks any central body, and for the most part anyone is free to slap a SHARP patch on their jacket and say they're a member of SHARP, when the truth is that there is no actual organization to be a member of.

In Europe, SHARP has expanded to include youths who are not skinheads, and members are closely aligned with the more politically active group Red Anarchist Skinheads (RASH).

RASH

One of the more obscure offshoots of the skinhead subculture is the Red Anarchist Skinheads (RASH). Through the music of British bands such as the Redskins and Oi Polloi, the rhetoric of socialism and working-class ideals was woven into the subculture; however, the strong nationalist leanings of skinhead values almost eclipsed these left-leaning themes. This attitude may have contributed to the relatively late arrival of left-wing skinhead organizations. One of the founding members of SHARP, Andre Schlesinger, says of the mid-1980s in New York:

> In those days, there were no Redskin crews or anything even close to that in NYC ... at around that time certain people in and around SHARP realized that there needed to be a more politicized alternative to SHARP or at least individuals who were willing to take a stronger and more general anti prejudice stance.

As Grover, a self-proclaimed redskin, remembered, "A skin named Dan Sabater came up with the acronym RASH some time in '92, with that as the umbrella organization and his local gang as the 'Mayday Crew' with several like-minded folks." According to the RASH website, the organization was officially founded in 1993 in New Jersey "as an international organization for skinheads who hold anti-fascist and radical left-wing political views." Grover moved to New York from Cincinnati to assist with establishing chapters across the United States. "I and others had some mixed success with establishing RASH crews around Cincinnati, Dayton, and Columbus, Ohio," he recalled. As he noted, "RASH was created in the USA, but has had a lot of trouble taking root, though it still might happen."

While this group is a minority in the skinhead subculture in the United States, RASH is a much larger movement in Europe. Its greater popularity there may be due to the existence of both Socialist and National Socialist parties holding office in many European countries. Holding left-wing beliefs has less stigma in these nations, and there appears to be a more immediate threat from far-right-wing groups.

Conclusion

The legacy of both the racist and antiracist organizations that were part of the skinhead subculture in the 1980s and 1990s has had a lasting impact. One of the most striking results of the politicization of American skinheads is the intense backlash against politics within the scene. As one skinhead in Chicago explains, "After a while it became like a witch-hunt. If someone didn't claim SHARP, they were automatically labeled a Nazi, or vice versa. Most skinheads wanted to be labeled as skinheads without injecting politics into it."

Likewise, many racist skinheads became disenchanted by the "Do as I say, not as I do" attitude that was prevalent in the White Power scene. As friends turned into informants and infighting became common, some of the most dedicated members tuned out the message of the movement. Between 1994 and 1996, there was an exodus of first-generation White Power skinheads away from racist organizations. In their place, a new generation emerged, whose members entered the scene because of the association between skinheads and white supremacy. This breed of racist rarely had knowledge of the skinhead subculture in the context of its British roots.

When people decided to label themselves as supporting either the White Power or the SHARP position, the scene became divided and politics became a huge part of the skinhead culture. For some skinheads, their decision to choose one side or the other resulted in serious consequences, including jail time or death.

Conclusion: The Future of the Skinhead Subculture

What does the future hold for the American skinhead scene? There is no clear answer. The scene continues to survive as a whole, but has endured many ebbs and flows. Overall, the American skinhead scene is alive but no longer thrives as it did in the late 1980s and 1990s, when many major cities could count their skinheads by the hundreds. For a multitude of reasons, the skinhead subculture does not seem to be an attractive option for many of today's youth. The closed nature of the scene and the elitism of many of its participants often make newcomers feel unwelcome. In addition, the media's continued focus on the racist minority within the subculture has cemented the public's view of skinheads as nothing more than a segment of the White Power movement. Many individuals are hesitant to be labeled racists simply because they adopt the skinhead subculture.

Today's teenagers are also not as likely to associate with a single subculture as they were a generation or two ago. With their constant exposure to new trends that evolve with the lightning speed of the Internet, the youth of today seem more inclined to experiment with several different styles rather than settle on just one. The fact that the skinhead subculture is still active around the world is an indication of its potential longevity; the clothing and music have remained popular for almost 30 years. While the total skinhead population has varied over the years, it appears to be a scene that, like punk, will endure for many years to come.

Musically speaking, the subculture has seen many changes as well. Hardcore has seen an increase in its popularity among skinheads during this decade, and Oi! continues to be very popular as well. Ska, which was popular among skinheads in the 1990s, has decreased in popularity, but "skinhead reggae" has surged in popularity in the past 10 years or so at the more traditional end of the scene. Punk in its various guises still has a place in the hearts and ears of some skinheads, and some also enjoy soul music (particularly Motown and Northern Soul). Racist skinheads who used to listen mostly to Oi! in the 1980s now are primarily into hardcore (especially a racist branch called "hatecore") and metal. Some styles of music are more popular with skinheads in some areas than in others, and there are also slight regional differences in the style of dress.

One thing many skinheads can agree on is that the subculture's future is in the hands of the young. While there are active American skinheads in their mid-40s who originally shaved their heads in the early 1980s, most no longer dress as skinheads, even though they maintain ties with the subculture. These older skinheads have settled into more normal lives, with family life and careers taking precedence over "hanging out" and scene activities. As a skinhead who is approaching his fortieth birthday says:

> Unlike many other youth-cult music scenes, I find it very easy to grow older as a skinhead. There's nothing that I can see that contradicts the identities of "skinhead" and "grown-up." Working hard and fulfilling your responsibilities have always been respected in the skinhead scene.

Another former skinhead states:

> I still love reggae, I buy Ben Sherman shirts whenever I'm in New York, and every once in a while when someone pisses me off I think, "Aren't you lucky you didn't meet me when I was sixteen?" Despite everything, it is still part of my personality twenty years down the road. I'm a middle school teacher in an urban school, and sometimes I see myself in some of my kids who are involved in gangs.

When reflecting on the importance of the subculture, certain elements will always ring true regardless of whether someone is still dressing or calling himself or herself a "skinhead." Roger Miret, lead singer of Agnostic Front summarizes this point well:

> Skinhead is in your heart. You don't have to shave your head or buy everything contained in a skinhead book. It's a movement you dedicate your life to and it includes working-class beliefs that I still teach to my children today.

Many skinheads, no matter which generation they belong to, believe the same.

Skinhead Snapshots: Notable Gangs, Bands, and Miscellaneous Aspects of the Subculture

It is impossible to cover the entirety of the skinhead subculture in just one book. There are so many variations and facets of the subculture beyond specific dates and cities. To provide a sampling of the many variations within the overall skinhead subculture, these snapshots of unique aspects of the scene give the reader an insider view of what one would find musically and culturally in different regions of the United States. The first snapshots provide details on the population of skinheads, including the role of women in the scene, skinheads of color, and the curious presence of minority skinheads who gravitated to the White Power movement. The next set of snapshots focuses on one of the most important aspects of the skinhead subculture—the development of crews and gangs. Similar to what has occurred in other subcultures involving gang affiliations, violence and aggression stemmed from these crews and helped shape the general public's definition of the term "skinhead." The last set of snapshots highlights the notable bands that contributed to the popularity of skinheads and gave birth to a new form of music in the United States.

Skinhead Girls

> "skinhead girl with all her pride, will never run will never hide"
> —"(She's a) Skinhead Girl Warrior" by Warzone

Females have been involved in the skinhead subculture since its inception; however, skinhead life has always been a male-dominated scene. The term "skinhead girl" is applied to women of all ages in the scene and has been used since the first generation in 1969. The term was immortalized in song by the band Symarip in its reggae classic, *Skinhead Girl*. In later years, other terms gained popularity, including "skin byrds," "knuckle girls," and "boot girls" to describe female skinheads.

Girls typically adopt the lifestyle by having skinhead boyfriends or a natural affinity to the music, violence, and the style. Some male skinheads are of the opinion that females do not play an equal role in the skinhead scene. Because of the culture's history of aggression and the mob mentality that exists within it, some skinheads do not see a role for women outside of girlfriend or wife. This way of thinking is particularly prominent among racist skinheads, who often view women as "breeders" for the white race, but it also exists among traditional skinheads. Conversely, many skinheads on both sides of the racial line view women as equals and welcome their participation in all areas of the scene.

On average, most females do not live the skinhead lifestyle longer than five to six years. In the United States, women who stay involved in the scene for more than five years are relatively rare, and even fewer still are active for more than ten years. In the United Kingdom and in Europe, there are many more women who keep the hairstyle and skinhead attire well into adulthood. The cause of this is twofold. First, upon entering the workforce, many skinheads are forced to grow their hair to assimilate to societal norms. Second, the dress options for female skinheads consist in large part of clothing modeled after menswear, which is sometimes a harsh look. As a result, female skinheads modify the traditional skinhead look—namely, by growing out their hair to soften their appearance and subsequently moving toward more feminine styles of dress.

Because the look and rituals of skinheads are based on masculine traits, the role of women in the subculture is not clearly defined and varies from city to city. Skinhead girls often find themselves walking a fine line between embracing the masculine traits of the subculture and maintaining their femininity. They are supposed to be tough and ready to stand up for themselves and their friends, but if they act too aggressively they can be viewed as being too "butch" or manly. Some cities have females who take a nurturing position in the scene and are sometimes referred to as "mama skins." Other female skinheads have taken proactive positions in their scenes by organizing events, publishing books, and producing films that cater to skinheads.

Non-white Skinheads

"You were a skinhead? How??! You're not even white!"

Despite the mainstream media's almost exclusive focus on the racist element of American skinheads, the ethnic make-up of the subculture is actually as varied as that of the country itself. Given the sometimes sensationalist press reports and the undeniable presence of racists within the scene, some wonder why people of color would want to become skinheads. Skinheads who are not white often have to defend their choice to people outside the scene. Greg Narvas describes the reaction of the general public when they encounter a non-white skinhead: "It's like telling someone I was from Mars."[1]

Because the roots of British skinheads were heavily derived from Jamaican rudeboys, there was a natural inclination for blacks to become involved with the U.K. subculture. As a result, there were black skinheads in the first and second generations of skinheads in England, even while the subculture was vilified in the press for attacking immigrants. Likewise, the demographics of American cities lent themselves to defining the majority group of skinheads geographically. Both Los Angeles and New York always had active skinheads of varied ethnicities. Freddy Madball explains of New York City, "Every skinhead we knew growing up in the Lower East Side was a different ethnic background. Black, white, Hispanic—every kind of skin you could think of."[2] Because the main tenets of the subculture are not based on race or politics, it was natural that nonracist white skinheads and skinheads of color would identify with the subculture. For this reason, the U.S. skinhead population continues to reflect the country's diversity despite the continued association of some elements of the subculture with racism.

In 1988, a thriving skinhead scene could be found in Oahu, Hawaii. This scene was made up of roughly 80 percent Hawaiian natives, and of those approximately 15 percent were white. Many of the natives were hapas (Hawaiian for "mixed race"), while the rest were a mélange of Chinese, Japanese, Filipino, and native Hawaiian.

When Perry Templar, an African American bassist for a popular skinhead band, became a skinhead in 1986, he recalled, "There were other black, Hispanic and Asian skinheads in Chicago at that time, so I never felt out of place because of my race." He continued, "Overall, race hasn't played much of a role in my life as a skinhead."

An African American woman from California describes becoming a skinhead in the mid 1980s:

> Being a black female skinhead in the '80s wasn't easy. I took an entire year before shaving my head because I wanted to make sure I understood what it was all about. The one thing I learned through the years is that by being a black skinhead I had to be willing to stand my ground and always ready to fight.

Today skinheads can be found all over the world, including in Southeast Asia and South America. Diversity is still present in the subculture, although the press largely focuses on the racist element of the subculture—namely, American racist organizations and the recent rise of racist skinheads in Russia.

The Nazis of Color

An anomaly of the skinhead subculture has been the existence of skinheads of color who attempt to align themselves with the White Power movement. Kevin, a black skinhead, recalls a Puerto Rican friend who proclaimed he was going to join the racist group WAR Skins. When Kevin questioned his non-white status, his friend replied, "I am Spanish, not Puerto Rican!"

There are several accounts of black skinheads who spewed racist rhetoric and got tattoos of swastikas and other racist images. Some did it to gain attention, while others were mentally impaired. More often, interracial skinheads with conflicting feelings about their heritage were not quite sure where they fit in. This phenomenon is not unique to the skinhead subculture but, in fact, has been documented in other racist organizations for decades. In the 1930s, Lawrence Dennis, a leader in the American Fascist Party, was a mixed-race man who passed for white.

This phenomenon has been documented even among the first and second generations of British skinheads. One former member of the National Front remembers a black youth who would apply to become a member of the organization every year. Phil Templar, a black skinhead, speculates, "Back in the early '80s in England you would see black skinheads 'Seig Heil-ing.' Why? To offend people or they were being paid by the photographers."

Perhaps the most extreme example of this kind of nonstandard racist affiliation took place in Florida. A young skinhead named John Daly joined a skinhead crew called the Aryan Youth Front. Later the group was absorbed by the Florida chapter of the American Front, which was headed by California transplant David Lynch. Daly was an active member of the organization—until it was revealed that he was Jewish. In an interview, he explained why he joined the American Front:

> Part of it was fear of what would happen to me if I quit, and part of it was that I was sixteen and not thinking clearly. I had gone from being this nerdy, bespectacled geek to being someone who, when I walked into a room, people cut a path. I commanded attention, and that was pretty cool. I liked it. I didn't want to give it up.[3]

When Daly's identity was discovered by other members of the American Front, Heather Arnold, his superior, ordered him to Daytona Beach to attend a party. Once he was there he was severely beaten and left for dead. Two members, Richie Myers and Robert Huttner, were charged with attempted second-degree murder and sentenced to 10 years in prison.

Whatever the reason for passing or affiliating with white supremacist organizations, the existence of skinheads who do so has always been a part of the subculture.

Gangs of New York

Because New York was home to one of the oldest skinhead scenes, it is not surprising that it was the first area to form established crews. The skinheads from the Lower East Side of Manhattan were the original crew in the city; this group included members from the bands Warzone, Cro-Mags, and Agnostic Front. The crew's reputation was hard, tough, and violent. It was not long before this first generation gave way to a more organized group of skinhead crews, however.

The Oxblood crew started off as a collection of friends, including two brothers and six other skinheads from the Jackson Heights area in Queens. By 1987, this group's size had tripled to 25 people; it later peaked at approximately 40.

Around the same time Oxblood began in Queens, another crew called the Uptown Bootboys (UBB) began. The crew was started in 1987 by four Puerto Rican skinheads from the Bronx. As one of the original members recalled, "We all would meet up for shows on the same subway line going downtown. So one thing led to another and we started calling ourselves the Uptown Bootboys." By the summer of 1988, the UBB had grown to 15 members. Members came from the Bronx (North and South), East Harlem, the Upper West Side, and Washington Heights. By 1997, the crew had ceased its activity, having lasted for nearly 10 years.

Perhaps the most well-known and long-lasting crew to come from New York was DMS. This group was started in late 1986 and emerged from Jackson Heights. The acronym DMS originally stood for "Doc Marten Stomp" or "Doc Marten Skinheads." This group was unique in that, reflective of New York's highly diverse culture, DMS was a merging of hip-hop, tagging, and hardcore subculture. While the crew's membership might not have resembled stereotypical skinheads, it embodied the brotherhood and spirit of the original Lower East Side crew. Members came from all the boroughs of New York. According to police records, the gang had a long history of fighting, assault, robbery, and even murder. This reputation was underscored in 1990 when members of DMS were involved in two separate assaults that resulted in murder. Four members were eventually given sentences of 25 years to life in prison for their crimes.

Despite these legal troubles, DMS still exists today, although now it is more aligned with the hardcore scene rather than with the skinhead scene. While the group started out as a skinhead crew, its acronym has come to mean many things, including "Drugs Money Sex" and "Dirty Money Syndicate."

Over the years, DMS members started bands, and soon the crew was associated with some of the most well-known New York hardcore bands. Currently, DMS exists to support a network of hardcore bands, including Vietnom, Madball, Skarhead, Agnostic Front, Rancid and Murphy's Law. The group includes rap acts La Coka Nostra and Danny Diablo and The Shotblockers, and hosts a weekly hardcore radio show called *Black n Blue*.

Gangland (Chicago)

True to the reputation of Chicago as "Gangland," skinheads in the city formed gangs almost immediately after the scene began. Unlike the gangs in New York, Chicago gangs were divided by racial beliefs and geographic locations. The first crew in Chicago was known as the Bomber Boys. This loosely organized crew of skinheads included biracial brothers Bob and Joe Matiljan, and two of the earliest skins, Sonny and Dwayne. As Dwayne remembers it, "The Bomber Boys included a bunch of us that started hanging out in 1980." While chapters of the Bomber Boys were eventually established in San Diego and Atlanta, the flagship crew in Chicago was defunct by the end of 1985.

Soon after the Bomber Boys disbanded, Skin Heads of Chicago (SHOC) was started by Sonny and another black skinhead, Corky. This group represented an alternative to the racist CASH and filled a void that the demise of the Bomber Boys left. SHOC consisted of skinheads from all races, including Latino and Filipino skinheads, and typified the rough image characteristic of Chicago, evidenced by a mix of skinhead style and gangster bravado. The crew members were known as much for their partying as for their hatred of Nazis.

Several other notable crews sprung up in Chicago throughout the years, most of which were affiliated with the organization known as Anti-Racist Action (ARA, also known as the Syndicate). Two of the more active affiliates under the ARA umbrella were the Northside Crew and Northern Indiana Skinheads (NISH). The Northside Crew comprised middle-class kids living on the North Side and in the northern suburbs of Chicago. NISH, however, was one of the more violent crews from 1988 until 1993. Due to its close proximity to racist strongholds in Indiana, NISH was known as the border patrol for Nazis between the borders of Indiana and Illinois. This crew was more closely aligned with non-skinhead street gangs than other crews in the area. Some members were also members of the Latin Kings while they also belonged to NISH. This gang affiliation was one of the catalysts that led to the group's demise: Problems with law enforcement led to a crackdown on NISH members, and the crew faded away by 1993.

With the decline of ARA and its affiliated crews, SHARP picked up where ARA left off. The Chicago chapter of SHARP was founded in 1989, based in the suburbs of Tinley Park. Members would venture to Chicago to distribute literature and go to shows. Some members of SHOC were wary of these suburban skinheads and did not appreciate their efforts in the city proper. However, SHARP was insistent and eventually found a home with skinheads in Blue Island. The Blue Island chapter of SHARP lasted until 1992.

Today Fear City, Chi-town Mafia Skins, and a revived version of SHOC are the active skinhead crews in Chicago. There are currently no active racist skinhead crews within the city limits. However, the nearby towns of Valparaiso, Chesterton, and Oceola, Indiana, are still havens for racists and have been the sites of Midwest "White Pride Fest" music festivals.

Southern California Crews

California's First Skinhead Crew: Toehead Army

The first documented skinhead crew in Los Angeles was called Toehead Army (THA). The name of the group—specifically the mis-spelling of the word "towhead"—was a play on the clean-shaven heads of its members. Jimbo, recalls, "I borrowed the name with permission from a punk crew of the same name but changed it to toehead". The founding members of the crew were Cliff, Sean (known as "Noosh"), and Jimbo. Cliff remembered, "It started out as a joke one night when we were at a club." Soon the name stuck, and by 1983 their small crew had grown from 15 skinheads to 40. "We were a crew of friends that enjoyed hanging out and having fun," Cliff continued. This crew associated with the Ska scene, and its style reflected the dress and lifestyle of the first-generation British skinheads. In addition to listening to 2Tone music, THA members were some of the first Southern California skinheads to listen to original Ska music from Jamaica. THA's primary hangout was Skinhead Alley, across the street from the all-ages club known as Haunted Studios.

Unlike most skinhead crews, Toehead Army members did not have a reputation of being violent unless provoked. While they were admittedly a closed group, they still welcomed the skinheads from nearby cities and transient skinheads from other states. Joel, a visiting skinhead from Santa Cruz, observed, "In 1985, L.A. seemed very gang oriented. While I was there I saw people get stabbed and shot at shows. By contrast, THA was fun and were the best Anglophile skinheads around." The same year that Joel moved to Los Angeles, three skinheads from Chicago also joined the scene. They brought with them racist rhetoric. Their entry marked the first time that racism had invaded this group of friends; as Cliff stated with distaste, "We never considered White Power skinheads as legitimate."

Eventually, members of THA moved away or stopped hanging out in Hollywood, although many of them remained close friends. In 2008, they had a reunion attended by more than 20 members. Some of the original THA members are still active in the skinhead scene, although they are now in their 40s. Regardless of their current lives, THA members have fond memories of their days as the first generation of traditional skinheads in Southern California.

Gang Warfare: Los Angeles's First Skinhead Gangs

One of the early skinhead gangs to appear in Southern California was called the Northside Firm (NSF), with members from South Pasadena, Alhambra, and San Gabriel Valley. NSF was formed in 1983 by Doug, who described the group's development this way: "We were skinheads down in Hollywood, and Los Angeles Death Squad (LADS), Fight For Freedom (FFF) and Suicidals were already there, and they started sweating skinheads. After all the fighting started going down, we started our own gang to protect ourselves." Other founding members of the crew included two biracial skinheads, Morgan and Scott Graham; the leader, Doug; a youth named Snake; and Richard from Alhambra.

Like THA, the early members of NSF hung out in Hollywood. They were primarily into the punk scene, although they hung out with THA as well. One NSF member Kevin recalled, "Toehead [members] were nicer guys that were into skinhead Moonstomp and all the reggae stuff. The Northside Firm was more into fighting, getting drunk, more fighting and getting laid."

In its height, Northside Firm had more than 100 members, organized in chapters in Alhambra, Monterey Park, South Pasadena, Pasadena, San Gabriel Valley, Monrovia, Arcadia, Duarte, and Covina. The group included both male and female members; the 20 female NSF members were from Alhambra and San Gabriel. These girls were not "jumped in" like males, but they were given gang names. In later years, the NSF membership included "cholos" (Latino gang members) and punk rockers. The violent reputation of NSF gained this organization the distinction of being one of the California skinhead crews mentioned in academic textbooks about gangs in Los Angeles.

The splintering of NSF resulted from infighting, drugs, and the growing number of Nazis in the West Covina area. Some members wanted to include Nazis in the crew, but Doug and other members, vehemently against Nazis, refused to let any of them join. The Northside Firm stopped being an active crew in 1989, and the void left by its demise was filled by racist skinhead gangs including the Order, American Front, and Reich Skins.

Along the coast, other gangs sprung up around Los Angeles; their members included a mix of Latino and white skinheads. One of the largest of these gangs was the Southbay Skins, which was first documented in 1985, when the group had more than 20 members. This crew was one of the first to have a mix of nonracist and racist members. One skinhead surmises, "This may have been from a lot of those guys being incarcerated for so long. There were Mexican guys in the crew and white guys." Some of them had swastika tattoos, while others talked about fighting against White Power crews from nearby Orange County. As the skinhead continued, "They were never an antiracist or hardcore Nazi gang; they eventually just turned into a criminal gang."

In 1986, Southside Los Angeles Death Squad (LADS) formed as an offshoot of the Hollywood LADS. Neither crew had much in common other than the name. The Hollywood LADS was a punk gang, while the Southside comprised primarily skinheads.

These early crews soon gave way to even more violent skinhead gangs, which were organized more like street gangs.

Los Angeles's Second Generation of Skinhead Gangs

By 1987, skinhead gangs across Southern California helped define the "gangsta skinhead" persona. The mixture of gang culture and the skinhead scene was almost exclusive to this region and was emulated by both racist and antiracist skinheads. Racist crews such as the Skinhead Dogs in Ventura County embodied the "gangsta skinhead" image as much as the antiracist groups. Several antiracist gangs contributed to this fusion of subcultures, including Carson Skins and Ghost Town Skins.

In 1989, a crew called Unity, originally a mix of punks and skinheads, emerged in the San Gabriel Valley (SGV). By the time Unity became known primarily as a skinhead crew, it had gained a reputation for fighting Nazi skinheads. By 1990, the group included 60 members. At its height of popularity, SGV Unity included almost 100 individuals from Pomona to El Monte to East Los Angeles.

In 1987, the Huntington Beach Skins were the first Orange County (OC) skinhead gang mentioned in the press. Their members were primarily white, but the group also had some Latino members. Its unofficial leader, who went by the name Peewee, told the *Los Angeles Times*, "No one goes around preaching white power."[4] At the time of the article's publication, the group had 25 members, including some females.

Another OC crew was called Crazy F*cking Skinheads (CFS); it included both white and Mexican American youths. Eventually, a half-dozen known crews existed in Orange County, including North West Orange County Skins (NWOC), La Habra Skins, Public Enemy Number One (PENI) Skins, and San Juan Skins. PENI Skins eventually abandoned skinhead-only membership and has become one of the most notorious White Power gangs in Southern California. Eventually some former OC skinheads joined other racist gangs such as the Nazi Lowriders.

By late 1987, skinheads in Orange County were primarily racist. The American Firm was the first skinhead crew to consciously adopt racist ideology.

Neighboring areas of Lake Elsinore and Riverside also had their share of skinheads. The city of Riverside was home to a large Ska scene and an even larger White Power scene. Eventually, the Orange County–based WAR Skins and PENI Skins started affiliate chapters in Lake Elsinore.

Farther south, San Diego Skinheads (SDSH) was one of the first recognized crews in the county. SDSH comprised Latino and white skinheads. Its chief rival was a punk gang called the Choir Boys. SDSH were hardcore skinheads who frequented punk shows.

Other crews in the area were the SD Bootboys, Bomber Boys, and North County Firm. Eventually, members of the Bootboys and Bomber Boys evolved into the San Diego chapter of WAR Skins.

Currently, most skinhead gangs from the 1980s and 1990s in California are inactive. Clashes between Nazis and antiracist groups are rare, with an uneasy geographic division separating the two groups. Some areas are known as either antiracist or White Power strongholds, and each group rarely crosses the other's boundaries. However, when the two groups have interacted, deadly consequences have ensued. Three skinhead deaths in Southern California were attributed to clashes between Nazis and antiracist crews between 2008 and 2009.

Northern California Crews

Teenage Warning: San Francisco Skinhead Crews

In the early 1980s, two crews of skinheads evolved from the local punk scene in San Francisco: the Bay Area Skinheads (BASH) and the SF Skins. The original BASH was made up of a core group of skinheads— Terry Bash, Bob Blitz (Bob Heick), and Curtis. From the beginning, skinhead girls were always a part of the SF scene. Summer and an Asian skinhead girl named Inky were two of the earliest skinhead girls, but eventually many girls claiming skinhead hung out and were collectively referred to as the BASH Girls.

SF Skins (also known as SF Skinz) was started a few months after BASH, when Mark Dagger began organizing local skinheads. Dagger was already known for being a scary figure in the punk scene; he was also the singer for the punk band Urban Assault. By 1985, both crews had discarded the punk look of leather jackets and adopted the look and values of English skinheads.

By the winter of 1985, BASH had faded away and SF Skins became the dominant crew on the Northern California scene. BASH and SF Skins had some racist members, even though initially both included skinheads of different races. It is rumored that the demise of the SF Skins came about when they caught the attention of the local Hell's Angels owing to the increased police presence attracted by the skinheads' criminal activities on Haight Street. It is reported that the SF Skins were told to join the Hell's Angels or disband. The crew dissolved in 1986. That same year, Bob Blitz from BASH started a new crew called American Front—the first racist crew in the Bay Area

Other Northern California Crews

Skinheads also spread to Sacramento, California's state capital. The first crew, the Death Heads, actually predated the SF Skins and BASH by a year, and was greatly influenced by the second-generation skinheads from the United Kingdom. A skinhead from Sacramento recalled, "[The Death Heads] were really into Oi and dressed like British skinheads." Later the Death Heads evolved into the Sacto Skins, who were largely nonracist and nonpolitical. By 1989, however, the Sacto Skins had racist members and quickly became as notorious as their counterparts in San Francisco.

The first skinhead crew in Santa Cruz was called the Foremost Firm—the name came from a local milk producer, Foremost Dairy Farms. One of the founding members, Morgan, moved to Santa Cruz from Pasadena, where he had been one of the first members of the Los Angeles–based Northside Firm. Like other early skinhead crews, the Foremost Firm was influenced by Oi! music and the punk scene in San Francisco. It is said that members of the Foremost Firm were the inspiration for the Camper Van Beethoven song, *Take the*

Skinheads Bowling. Eventually, the Foremost Firm grew in size to include 10 members, who would travel to San Francisco and often interacted with BASH.

By 1987, after a split between the punk and traditional members, the remains of the Foremost Firm joined with another mod/skinhead crew called the Perry Boys and began to call themselves the Centurions— a joke based on the Meatmen's punk song, *Centurions of Rome*. There was never a large racist element in Santa Cruz, as it was dominated by the "traditional skinhead" population.

Ultraviolance: Skinheads in Portland

Skinheads were first documented in Portland, Oregon, in 1985, when two brothers from England started a crew called PUSH, or Portland United Skinheads. Like many of the skinhead crews emerging in other cities throughout the United States at the time, PUSH was an apolitical group, but it included both racist and nonracist members. Soon this group was replaced by two other crews, Preservation of the White American Race (POWAR) and East Side White Pride (ESWP), which were decidedly racist. The latter crew was involved in the beating of an immigrant college student, Mulugeta Seraw. After this racially motivated death, Portland was inundated with racist skinheads who moved into the area. Soon Portland gained a reputation for being a good city in which to find like-minded people and racist skinheads from San Francisco, Tulsa, Orlando, and Dallas, moved to the area.

One organization emerged from the void left by the demise of POWAR and ESWP in the aftermath of the Mulugeta Seraw trial. The Nationalist Socialist Front (NSF), headed by Randy Krager was founded in 1994. Eventually NSF became Volksfront, one of the longest-standing racist groups in the region.

To combat the growing racist population, skinheads from ARA in Chicago and Minneapolis moved to Portland to assist with the organization of antiracist skinheads. As a result, during the early 1990s, an unprecedented escalation of violence between the local SHARP crew and rival white supremacist groups occurred. As one antiracist skinhead remembers, "Every show was a riot, there were all-out fights on the street, homes got invaded—it was a war."

The fighting came to a head on New Year's Eve in 1992. According to the Portland Police, the two groups arranged to meet to settle their differences. A shooting occurred in a snow-covered parking lot. The victim, Erik Banks, died of a gunshot wound to the face; he was declared dead on arrival at Portland Adventist Hospital shortly after the shooting. Erik Banks, a recent arrival to the city, was a Hammerskin from Minnesota and the former lead singer of the popular White Power band Bound for Glory. His killer was charged with first-degree manslaughter and sentenced to five years in prison. By contrast, in 1988, the racist skinhead convicted of murdering Mulugeta Seraw was sentenced to life in prison. Racist skinheads have turned Erik Banks into a martyr and point to the disparate prison terms as evidence of their persecution.

Today, Rose City Bower Boys ("Rose City" is Portland's nickname) are one of the only nonracist crews left in the city of Portland, it celebrated their 15-year anniversary in 2009. By comparison, Volksfront has the largest presence in the Pacific Northwest in the White Power scene. This group was recently featured in the television series *Gangland*. With chapters across the United States as well as in Europe, Volksfront has been identified the Southern Poverty Law Center as one of the largest skinhead hate groups still active in America.

Skinhead Invasion: Noncontinental U.S. Skinheads

Puerto Rico Skinheads

Given that New York has such a large Puerto Rican community, it is only natural that many skinheads there have been of Puerto Rican descent. As a result of the frequent emigration between the two areas, a mirror skinhead scene emerged in Puerto Rico in the early 1990s. Skinheads hung out at La Tea, a local club in San Juan. Puerto Rico even had a skinhead band called Al Raz (Spanish for "close shave"); the band stated that it was influenced by the British sound. The crew on the island was called CPPR, or Cabeza de Piel De Puerto Rico ("Skinheads of Puerto Rico"); it had chapters in Florida as well as New York. To this day, crews such as DMS (New York) and Color

Blind Crew (Florida) have members with Puerto Rican roots in their ranks.

Hawaii Skinheads

The origins of skinheads in Hawaii can be traced to military transients and islanders visiting the mainland. Around 1986, a well-known punk went to the mainland; when he returned as a skinhead, the subculture was introduced in Oahu. As Nos, a longtime skinhead recalls, "Carlos was a charismatic guy, so a lot of the tougher punks shaved their heads and became skinheads, too." Because of the adversarial nature between punks and many of the locals, skinheads took a role in being the protectors of the scene. By 1988, a newer set of skinheads had sprung up. This second generation subscribed more to the British skinhead style and music.

The first organized crew in Hawaii started in 1987 and called itself HARSH (Hawaiian Antiracist Skinheads) as a reaction to the negative media coverage attached to the skinhead movement. The group included skinheads as well as punks, and remained active until 1990. Occasionally, transient members from the military had White Power leanings. Three or four of them formed a crew in an effort to protect themselves from the local skinheads. Their efforts were largely ridiculed, and today the racist element of skinheads in Hawaii is virtually nonexistent.

The last crew to appear on the island was originally called F*cking Chaos Skins (FCS), but later changed its name to Fist City Skins. There are still FCS members present in Hawaii, though they are now in their 30s. As one member joked, "Now we are a secret society with secret handshakes, secret language and secret agendas."

CASH: The First White Supremacist Skinheads

CASH (Chicago Area Skinheads) is recognized as one of the first organized white supremacist skinhead groups in the United States. Its leader, Clark Martell, is probably one of the most controversial figures in the Chicago skinhead scene. He first arrived in the Chicago punk scene in 1983, after serving a four–year prison sentence for "attempting to commit aggravated arson against a Hispanic Person." While in prison, Martell was diagnosed with a serious mental illness, which might account for his odd behavior in subsequent years. In September 1984, shortly after his release, he was arrested again for defacing property with racist symbols. Before he adopted the skinhead style, Martell was a member of the American Nazi Party.

By 1985, the 25-year-old Martell had begun referring to himself as a skinhead. He took an active role in perpetuating the agenda of racist skinheads from Britain. He adopted the name Romantic Violence for his music and T-shirt distribution business. Martell was one of the first American distributors of Skrewdriver records. In 1985, CASH members started a band called Final Solution; it was one of the first documented American bands with overtly racist lyrics.

CASH members largely came from the suburbs surrounding Chicago. A large amount of their time was spent at Martell's apartment in Blue Island. Dwayne, one of the original skinheads in Chicago, concedes that part of the reason Martell got large numbers of members in his group so quickly was the fact that skinheads from the city of Chicago did not welcome skinheads from the suburbs. The latter skinheads, referred to as "weekend warriors," came out to the city only for shows and quickly retreated to the suburbs once they were over. To create CASH, Martell targeted disenfranchised teens who were eager to hang out with anyone accepting of them; he would invite them over to his apartment and introduce them to racist ideology.

Martell had an extensive police record; his most prominent charge stemmed from an act of revenge directed at a "race traitor." Martell, his girlfriend, and four other members of CASH broke into a skinhead girl's apartment, beat her, and left the phrase "race traitor" written on the wall in her blood. According to the Assistant State's Attorney Tony Calabrese, the victim was soaked with her own blood and both of her eyes were swollen shut.[5] The guilty CASH members were arrested in 1988. Martell was sentenced to 11 years in prison in June 1989.

A second generation of CASH developed after Martell went to prison. They recruited disaffected skaters and punks much as Martell had done almost a decade earlier. The New CASH revolved around the band White American Youth (WAY), who's members later changed its name to Final Solution in homage to the original band made up of first-generation CASH members. By the mid-1990s, the crew became inactive for good when members started to leave the scene.

Bands

Agnostic Front

Considered one of the most influential hardcore bands ever, Agnostic Front—the New York City band formed in late 1980 by guitarist Vinnie Stigma—started out as a skinhead band playing simple punk/thrash music and quickly made a name for itself in the New York punk scene. After going through several vocalists, the group settled on Roger Miret as front man in 1982. In 1983, the band released its debut EP called *United Blood*, which is now one of the most highly sought-after collector's items among hardcore fans. Their debut LP, 1984's *Victim in Pain*, is perhaps one of the most influential hardcore punk albums to this day. In 1983, punk rock magazines accused Agnostic Front of being racist (although singer Miret is of Cuban descent) due to its Iron Cross logo and criticism of public assistance.

After more line-up changes, Agnostic Front changed its musical style to a more metal direction. This trend began with the group's 1986 LP *Cause for Alarm* and continued until the band called it quits in 1992.

Stigma and Miret re-formed Agnostic Front in 1997 and have continued to tour and record ever since. The band's first three albums since this comeback—*Something's Gotta Give, Riot Riot Upstart*, and *Dead Yuppies*—had a hardcore punk/Oi! sound reminiscent of its early days, while the two latest albums—*Another Voice* and *Warriors*—have a more modern hardcore/metal sound. Agnostic Front's live show continues to be as intense as ever. The band has maintained a large and devoted following worldwide, consisting of both skinhead and non-skinhead fans.

Anti-Heroes

Atlanta's the Anti-Heroes remains one of the most popular most influential American Oi! bands dating from the late 1980s and

1990s. It was the first American Oi! band to release an album and also the first to tour in Europe.

The band was formed in 1985 by Mark Noah and guitarist Joe Winograd. After a line-up change, they soon settled on Mike Jones on bass and Tim Spier on drums. The Anti-Heroes released its first album, *That's Right*, in 1987 on the English label Link Records, which helped it gain a large following among skinheads and Oi! fans on both sides of the Atlantic. The band followed this effort up with 1988's *Don't Tread on Me*, which is considered by most skinheads to be an American Oi! classic.

The band split up in 1990, but Mark Noah soon re-formed the band in 1993 with British-born guitarist Mark MaGee (formerly of The Glory and Condemned 84), Mike Jones back on bass. and new drummer Phil Soloman. This line-up released several great records, most notably 1996's *American Pie* CD, before Phil Soloman was replaced on drums by Don Shumate.

The Anti-Heroes finally disbanded in 2001, but its contributions to the growth of the U.S. Oi! live on.

Cro-Mags

Along with Agnostic Front, the members of the Cro-Mags are largely considered to be the founders of the NYHC (New York Hardcore) music scene, and their debut album, *The Age of Quarrel*, is considered a classic of the genre. The band was formed in New York City in 1980 by Harley Flanagan. The group went through various line-up changes before settling on John Joseph (vocals), Harley Flanagan (bass), Parris Mitchell Mayhew (guitar), and Mackie Jayson (drums). It added Doug Holland on rhythm guitar in 1985, creating what is considered by most to be the definitive Cro-Mags line-up. The band then released its classic *Age of Quarrel* album in 1986. A record that was as influential in heavy metal circles as in hardcore punk ones, it remains the band's crowning glory.

After several worldwide tours, singer John Joseph left and Harley took over on vocals as well as bass. The Cro-Mags also replaced drummer Mackie Jayson with Petey Hines and released its second LP, *Best Wishes*. This album had a more heavy metal feel to it, which alienated some of the group's hardcore and skinhead fan base. The

Cro-Mags continued to record with various line-ups throughout the 1990s and 2000s and released several albums, one of which (*Revenge*) harkened back to the group's early hardcore punk feel.

The Templars

The Templars are, without a doubt, one of the most unique bands to come out of the American skinhead scene. Formed in Long Island, New York, in April 1991, the band stood out from the rest with its mixed-race line-up and diverse array of musical influences. The band's sound owes as much to the early sound of the Who and the Rolling Stones as it does to anything punk and Oi! related. The Templars' original line-up consisted of Carl Templar (Carl Fritscher) on guitar and vocals, Phil Templar (Phil Rigaud) on drums, and Don Templar (Don Gerle) on bass.

The Templars were named after an ancient order of Christian knights called the Knights Templar, which were prevalent in Europe during the 1100s to 1300s. Many Templars record and song titles are based on the history of the Knights Templar.

The band began playing gigs in 1992 and quickly built a solid following on the East Coast. Once its debut album, *The Return of Jacques de Molay*, was released in 1994, the group's following spread worldwide.

The Templars experienced their first line-up change in 1996, with Perry replacing Don on bass. In the late 1990s, the band released many recordings and played across the United States, Canada, and Europe. It added a rhythm guitarist named Chet Knight for live shows in 2000. The group members produced all of their records themselves in their own Acre Studios, with Carl playing all the guitar and bass tracks and providing the vocals, and Phil handling the drums (the only exceptions being 1999's *Omne Datum Optimum* and 2001's *Horns of Hattin* CDs). In 2004, Matt replaced Perry on bass; Perry returned to the fold in 2006. In 2007, Chris replaced Chet on rhythm guitar, and the band has been playing sporadic gigs across the United States and Europe ever since. A new album is now in the works, which should be released in 2012.

The Toasters

New York City's Toasters are the longest-running Ska band in the United States, with a career spanning more than 25 years, although singer/guitarist Robert "Bucket" Hingley is the only original member. Formed in New York City by the British Hingley in 1981, the Toasters arrived onto the Lower East Side scene. The group is one of the original bands cited as part of the "third wave" of Ska, which brought bands such as No Doubt and the Mighty Mighty Bosstones to the public's attention in the mid-1990s. To date, The Toasters have released nine albums, most of them on Hingley's Moon-Ska label. This band's music has been featured in TV shows such as *Mission Hill* and *KaBlam!*, and the group has recorded music for several TV commercials, including one for America Online. Despite numerous line-up changes, The Toasters continue to tour around the world and celebrated their 25th anniversary in 2007 with the release of the album *One More Bullet*.

Notes

1. Interview, *L.A. Retrospective: Mod and Skinhead Scenes. Part One*, 2008. Available at http:/leytonbuzzards.wordpress.com.
2. Interview, Frank151, Chapter 33: DMS, 2008. Available at http:/www.frank 151.com/book/chap33.
3. *A Skinhead's Secret Intelligence Report* 122 (Summer 2006). Available at http:/ www.splcenter.org retrieved, accessed November 10, 2010.
4. Dennis McLellan, "Ganging Up: 'Skinhead' Groups of White Youths Appear on Rise," *Los Angeles Times (Orange County Edition)* (November 30, 1987), 1.
5. Matt O'Connor, "Skinhead Leader Beat Up Ex-Girlfriend, Prosecution Tells Jury," *Chicago Tribune* (April 27, 1989), 3.

Glossary

14/88: A racist skinhead term: The 14 refers to the 14 words "we must secure the existence of our people and a future for white children"—a quote from David Lane of the white supremacist paramilitary group the Order. The 88 refers to the letter "h," which is the eighth letter of the alphabet; it is code for "Heil Hitler."

54–46: The prison number referenced in a reggae song by the Maytals. Skinheads often wrote this term as graffiti.

Agnostic Front: Famous hardcore band from New York City. It originally had an all-skinhead line-up and was one of the bands responsible for spreading the skinhead idea throughout the United States through touring. The group remains popular within the skinhead scene today.

American Front: Racist skinhead group founded in San Francisco, which existed during the late 1980s. It was led by Bob Heick, who was one of the skinheads involved in the fight on the *Geraldo Rivera Show*.

ARA: Anti-Racist Action. This group was started by skinheads from Minneapolis in the late 1980s, and branches soon sprang up throughout the United States. This group still exists today but is not exclusively skinhead in membership.

Aryanfest: White Power skinhead gathering that first took place in 1988 in Oklahoma. Occasional gatherings still take place today and are usually held in rural areas.

Ben Sherman: Brand of a shirt with a button-down collar, pleat in the back, and buttons on the back collar and sleeves. This brand first became popular with British mods and skinheads in the late 1960s and is still manufactured today.

Bomber jacket: Perhaps the most popular style of jacket among American skinheads. It is more commonly referred to as a flight jacket. The U.S. Air Force jacket comes with bright orange lining and in a wide variety of colors, with black and olive green being the most commonly worn by skinheads.

Bonehead: Derisive term widely used by nonracist skinheads to describe their racist counterparts. This term was first used among skinheads in London in the late 1970s but without any racial connotations at that time.

Bootboy: A British subculture that began in the early 1970s. Bootboys had medium-length or longer hair but often wore Doc Marten boots—hence the name. Skinheads from the late 1970s through today sometimes refer to themselves as bootboys, and many original bootboys were skinheads. They were often associated with gang violence that usually centered on soccer or neighborhood rivalries.

Boot party: A group of skinheads kicking someone on the ground in a fight. Boots are a favorite weapon among skinheads, and they often fight in groups.

Bovver: British slang term for violence.

Braces: The British term for suspenders. They were worn more for style than for holding up one's pants.

CASH: Chicago Area Skinheads. CASH was a racist skinhead group from Chicago that existed from the mid-1980s to the early 1990s. It was one of the first organized racist skinhead crews in the United States.

Chelsea: Skinhead girl's hairstyle, characterized by short cropped hair on top, bangs in front, and long pieces on the sides in front of the ears.

Cro-Mags: A popular New York City hardcore band that featured one of America's first skinheads, Harley Flanagan, on bass. Its first album, 1986's *The Age of Quarrel,* is considered a classic among skinheads and hardcore fans around the world.

Dickies: Line of workwear. The unpleated work pants are commonly worn by skinheads in Southern California and elsewhere. The Eisenhower jackets are sometimes worn as well. Pants are often tapered at the bottom for a more fitted look.

Doc Marten: British shoe company whose 1460 boot was made famous by skinheads in the 1960s and 1970s.

Feathercut: Skinhead girl's haircut that is longer and more subtle than the fringe or Chelsea. This style is worn mostly by skinhead girls who have been around long enough to have grown their hair out.

Fencewalker: Term used by both racist and antiracist skinheads to describe someone who does not want to take sides on issues of racism and/or politics.

Fred Perry: A line of sports and casual wear named after the famous British tennis player. The short-sleeved polo shirts first caught on with British mods in the 1960s and soon became standard skinhead issue as well. Fred Perry's famous laurel wreath logo also commonly appears as a tattoo among skinheads.

Freshcut: A new skinhead freshly shaved in, as the name implies; also, a skinhead with very little knowledge of the subculture's traditions and history. Such individuals are usually bullied or picked on by older skinheads until they gain respect from the other group members.

Fringe: Skinhead girl's haircut, featuring hair shaved very close on top with a #1 or #2 guard, short bangs, and the hair in back either worn the same length as on top or slightly longer in the back.

Hammerskins: Racist skinhead crew that began in Dallas, Texas, in 1986 as the Confederate Hammerskins. There are now Hammerskin branches throughout the United States as well as in several European countries. In the United States, different crews are grouped into regions, such as the Eastern Hammerskins, Western Hammerskins, and Northern Hammerskins, with those in the South keeping the original name.

Hardcore: A faster, harder form of punk rock that started around 1980 in cities such as Los Angeles, Boston, and Washington, D.C.

Hooligan: A term typically used to refer to a fanatical soccer fan. (Soccer is a very popular sport with skinheads worldwide.) Many skinheads refer to themselves as hooligans to show their appetite for violence and aggression.

Last Resort: (1) A famous skinhead shop in the East End of London that operated between 1980 and 1984. (2) An Oi! band from England that became one of the most influential bands of the genre.

Mod: The predecessor subculture to skinheads in England. Mods were fond of reggae, American soul, and early British pop bands such as the Who and Rolling Stones. They rode Vespa and Lambretta scooters and were obsessed with smart fashion.

Northern Soul: A British term for American soul music that became popular, particularly in Northern England, in the 1960s and 970s. It peaked in popularity in the mid-1970s and enjoyed a renewed popularity with the mod and skinhead revivals of the late 1970s.

Oi boy: A male who prefers Oi! music to the more "traditional" skinhead sounds of reggae and soul.

Oi! music: A subgenre of punk rock that is often associated with skinheads.

Oi toy: A girl who sleeps around indiscriminately with larger numbers of skinheads.

Paki bashing: A term coined in the 1960s in England when skinheads roamed areas of London and vandalized or beat up East Indian immigrants. In the United States, this term was sometimes used to describe beating up minorities.

RAHOWA: Racial Holy War; a racist band from Toronto, Canada, that was active in the 1990s.

Redskins: Skinheads who have far-left or communist political beliefs, and oftentimes are associated with the SHARP movement as well.

Rock Against Communism (RAC): Originally a concert series featuring white power bands, it eventually became a label for nationalist bands al over the world. Frequently bands labeled as RAC are racist or hold extreme right wing political views.

Rudeboy: A subculture with origins in the poorer section of Kingston, Jamaica, that began in the early 1960s. Rudeboys' style consisted of single-breasted suits, thin ties, porkpie hats, and sharp shoes. Their music of choice was Ska and reggae played in the local dancehalls and youth clubs. The rudeboy style was a major influence on the original skinheads in Britain.

SHARP: Skinheads Against Racial Prejudice; an organization established in New York City in 1988 by antiracist skinheads who wanted to make the point that all skinheads were not racist.

Ska: A style of music that was born in Jamaica. As Jamaicans started to immigrate to the United States in large numbers in the 1960s, Ska became popular first with mods and later with skinheads.

Skinbyrd: Slang term for a female skinhead. This term is widely used in America but not in Britain, even though "bird" is a traditional British slang term. "Bird" is most often spelled "byrd" in this context.

Skinhead reggae: Reggae music that catered to the skinheads in late 1960s Britain. The Trojan and Pama record labels and their many subsidiaries produced many records aimed specifically at skinheads. *Skinhead Moonstomp* by Symarip is but one example.

Skrewdriver: One of the first racist skinhead bands, and undoubtedly the most popular of these groups. Skrewdriver was a British punk band whose members adopted the skinhead look in an attempt to stand out from the rest of the punk scene. The band released several records in the late 1970s that were not racist in nature, even though singer Ian Stuart was already involved in racist politics. Skrewdriver went public as a racist band with the release of the *White Power* single in 1983. It gained a worldwide following among racist skinheads as well as with nonracists who enjoyed the group's music while disagreeing with their political views. Skrewdriver remained active until 1993, when Ian Stuart was killed in a car crash.

Smoothie: The final evolution of skinhead style in early 1970s Britain. Smoothie style appeared very normal to most observers but was a distinct style. The name "smooth" came from a hairstyle that was short on top and collar length in back and on the sides. Smoothie fashion was more casual than the suedehead, with round-collared shirts, corduroy pants, and plain shoes or patterned shoes called Norwegians being commonly worn. It was a short-lived subculture, which had all but disappeared by 1973.

Sort: A female smoothie.

Sta-Prest: Style of trousers made by Levi's in the 1960s. The name stems from the fact that the pants kept their crease after washing and did not need to be ironed. They were popular nighttime wear with skinheads in the 1960s and are still highly sought after today. Many American skinheads wear the cheaper and much more widely available Dickies workpants as a substitute of sorts.

Suedehead: A youth subculture that was an evolutionary branch off the original skinheads. Suedehead style was characterized by hair that was still short but was long enough to comb; suedehead girls wore their hair longer, too. Commonly worn fashion items included loafers, Levi's, Sta-Prest pants, Ben Sherman shirts, and Harrington jackets. Three-button single-breasted suits and Crombie overcoats were common nighttime wear. Suedehead emerged as a distinct style around 1970 in London. By 1972, it had largely given way to the smoothie style.

Traditional: A skinhead who prefers the original styles of skinhead fashion and music and often refers to the term "spirit of 69" when defining his or her lifestyle and beliefs.

Two-Tone (2Tone): A British record label that operated between 1979 and 1985. It released records by influential Ska revival bands such as The Specials, Selecter, and Madness, many of which were chart hits in the United Kingdom.

WAR: White Aryan Resistance; a racist organization founded by former Ku Klux Klan leader Tom Metzger in the 1980s. It gained notoriety as the first racist group to actively recruit skinheads into its ranks.

Primary Documents

Document 1

In the early 1980s, there were very few American skinhead girls. This is an account of an early skinhead girl from California who experienced both the U.S. and British skinhead scenes when they were at their height of popularity. Used by permission.

The Early Days of a Skinhead Girl

Essay by Bobbi Perez, Skinhead Girl from California

Becoming a "skinhead" was not an instantaneous thing for me, and the only reason I probably became a "skinhead" at all was because of my friends. The skin scene was new, and completely different from anything I had ever known before. It was tight, we were united, a bit wacky, and we really knew how to have a great time. Since 1980 I had been a punk and I had listened to Oi and TwoTone music coming from England. I knew what English skins looked like, but I did not understand the ideology of Skinhead.

For me, it all began when an exchange student from Sweden moved in with my family during high school. That year, 1979–80, growing up in a small beach town in Southern California may sound like heaven to some, but it was hell to me. The world was a different place then, music was crap, style and fashion were at an all-time low, life just drifted on an endless wave of monotony. Then this Scandinavian girl shows up, literally on my doorstep, and brought with her this incredible music. Those lovely vinyl records that changed my life forever . . . we listened to The Clash, Madness, The Specials, The Boomtown Rats, The Sex Pistols, The Undertones, Sham 69, The Boys. We played them over and over; it was pure inspiration.

And more than just the music, she introduced me to a whole new attitude toward the world around me. The only disappointment I remember during her stay was when she went to see Sham 69 live at the Whiskey a Go Go in L.A., and my parents wouldn't let me go. I vowed from that moment on I would not get left behind. When she returned home, I jumped into the punk scene full throttle.

My friend and I quickly became a part of the growing L.A. Hardcore scene. Even our own little quiet beach town, Santa Barbara, had a scene. We would hang out on State Street, a bunch of crazy-looking kids brought together by our desire to be different. We would parade around, acting belligerent, drinking booze out of soda cans, being obnoxious, creating our visible statement of nonconformity. At any given moment we would pile in my car and drive to wherever a show or gathering might be, whether it was Los Angeles, San Diego, San Francisco, or preferably somewhere closer to home. In the beginning I don't remember much deviation between the groups (skins/punks/mods); I don't think the numbers were large enough . . . we all congregated together, learning about music and scenes from one another.

The history of the various music scenes was hard to come by in the early '80s, especially in Southern California. We learned what we could from printed material coming out of Europe, but for the most part we were just creating our own scene.

When the movie *Dance Craze* came out, I thought I had died and gone to heaven. Everyone would get up and dance in the aisle/on stage; I knew this was the scene I wanted to be a part of. At the time the skin scene was so small. California had a Hardcore scene and the guys usually shaved their heads, wore boots, occasionally wore braces, and some even called themselves skins, but it wasn't the same.

During the summer of 1982 I went to England with my girlfriend. We were in a music shop in London when I came across a copy of *The Last Resort Album*. I was completely clueless, but the sales guy told me about the Last Resort shop, so my girlfriend and I wandered off in search of it. It was a weekday and pretty quiet at the market where the shop was located. As we approached it there were a couple of skins hanging about. They gave us hassle for looking "too punk." (Luckily my parents had been worried about my traveling with crazy punk hair so I had cut it short and bleached it.) The skins at the shop made me laugh, but my friend didn't like them at all. I bought some boots but they had to be ordered, so I needed to return on the weekend to pick them up. My friend refused to go back, so that Saturday I went on my own. When I turned the corner toward the shop, there were about 50 skins outside, and the inside was packed. There was a soccer match on that day and I guess ignorance is bliss, I just walked right through the crowd to the counter, picked up my boots, and left. I got a lot of looks, especially from the skin girls, but the guy who ran the shop was a real sweetheart, and secretly I dug the whole experience... it was way cool. When I got back to the U.S., I couldn't relate my English "skin" experience to my U.S. scene. Most of the skinhead clothes and boots I bought drifted to the back of my closet.

A few months later, maybe even a year, my friend Becca pulled out my Doc's (Doc Martens boots) from the closet and asked if she could borrow them. She was really into the skin thing. Then my old friend Rene, who was probably the first real skin I had ever known, brought this skin girl to our town. Slowly the skins started coming about, and it wasn't long before I started keeping my hair shaved with fringe, wearing Fred Perry's with mini-skirts, fishnets, and boots. I think we were fairly Neanderthal in our understanding of what it was to really be a skin, but it was great to have a bond, as it were, with your mates. The kids who piled in my car were now skins, and we would blast Cock Sparrer, The Toy Dolls, even the first album of Skrewdriver on my cassette player as we drove to L.A. to meet up with other skins. The skins who congregated in L.A. called themselves THA. They came from all over Southern California, and together we would drink at pubs, in alleys, at concerts and dance venues. There was no Internet, no email, and no cell phones, but somehow we found each other and quickly I became more knowledgeable about what it was to be a skin.

Occasionally, I would go visit friends in San Francisco, but they had a notoriously bad scene going on there. I had met some of the SF Skins and BASH Boys on an individual basis. My experience one on one had always been alright, but I loathed the stories I heard about the group as a whole—total, stupid thuggery in my opinion. One of my old friends from Santa Barbara had moved to San Francisco and he met and fell in love with a girl from the BASH scene. They got married and had what I first knew of as a "skinhead wedding." The bride did walk down the aisle to *Skinhead Girl*, and yes, it was the Oppressed version.

Back in L.A., skins from the rest of the U.S. started pouring in. I am not exactly sure why they came, but these skins were just as thuggish and bonehead as those in San Francisco. I was also beginning to hear stories that the San Diego scene was getting all creepy and Nazi-like. I had a friend who had gotten a tattoo of his San Diego Skin Scene on his forearm, but he had it removed when their scene began to attract racist thugs. I liked the skin scene for the style, the music, the dancing, and the drinking. Now L.A. was becoming infiltrated with racist skins, skins who wanted to fight against and amongst us. Then there were the media. The KKK started recruiting young thugs, shaving their heads and calling them skins. And there was the Geraldo incident . . . everything just started falling apart. I remember hearing some comment by Tom Metzger, the WAR guy, where he told the media in reference to skins, "Give them a beer and they will follow you anywhere." I always thought it was true, in a sad sort of way.

By now it was 1985, and I wanted to get out of L.A., out of the U.S., and return to London. I wanted to go back where it had all really started for me, maybe find some of that original feeling. As a hairstylist, I found a two-week hair education course in London and told my family I was planning to save up and attend.

The part I didn't tell my family was that I was hoping to get a job and stay there. My sister had done some traveling in Europe and as a gift gave me a two-month Eurail pass, which was totally awesome. So my roommate and I went on vacation to Amsterdam and Paris, where I managed to find skins pretty easily. Then in London my roommate left and I started hair school. One day after class I was at Carnaby Street, where I stumbled upon an American skin girl who was living in Brixton. It turned out she was from California as well and needless to say we hit it off, and she invited me to share her flat while I looked for a job.

We had a great time, going to clubs and pubs, seeing The Business and Desmond Decker. We went on Scooter Weekends to Margate and Isle of Wight. We truly had a blast.

When I got back to California, my old skin scene was all but gone; only a few of my friends remained. Most had moved on to other scenes. The Swing thing was the new scene, and I grudgingly began to cross over, growing my hair and lengthening my skirts. My girl friend in London said things had gotten bad there as well—the casuals were constantly fighting with the skins—and she was now basically a scooter girl.

I found some younger friends who represented the new skin scene in L.A. Then a group calling themselves Sharp Skins started to take root; they seemed to be fighting back against the Nazis and trying to reclaim what skinhead was all about.

I felt like my skin days were numbered, but I still loved to go to the scooter events and shows and dances when I could. It was now getting to be the late '80s and it seemed like I had to hang up my boots, but I really didn't want to. I went back to college and I guess I slowly started to grow up.

Documents 2 and 3

These are excerpts from interviews with the New York Oi! band Oxblood and Detroit Oi! band Pist'N'Broke. Both interviews first appeared in the fanzine Carry No Banners *in 1994. The interview with Oxblood captures the shift of the New York skinhead scene from hardcore to traditional Oi! sound of the time. The second interview provides insight into the skinhead scene from the perspective of those living in the Midwest.*

Oxblood

Would you give us a brief history of the band?
Oxblood was started at the beginning of 1992. Our demo was put out in September of that year. We just got our debut 7 called *Under the Boot* released in August on Headache Records. We're on the SPE

compilation *Only Spirit Is Unity* and should be on *U.S. of Oi! Volume II*. We played both D.C. Oi fests, and Boston a couple times, but most of our gigs are in NYC (New York City) and NJ (New Jersey).

Who are your influences and favorite bands?
We are influenced by a lot of early '80s street punk, from Criminal Class to Major Accident. There are many great bands we like. I'm also into the psychobilly scene a lot.

Years ago, skinheads in NYC were mostly associated with the hardcore scene. How do you feel about hardcore and does it still have an influence on NYC skins?
Years ago, NYC skins were definitely into the hardcore scene. There weren't really any Oi bands about then. This is the '90s and things have changed. Skins still go to hardcore shows, but it mainly appeals to the baggy pants–club–homeboy crowd. I can't speak for every skin, but from what I see most skins are mainly into Oi and Ska. As for myself, I was never really into hardcore except for some old classic stuff.

You just released your first record on the Headache label. Are you pleased with the result?
We are pleased with the result of our 7 on Headache, and from what I hear it's doing pretty good all over. Armen is a good guy to work with and he gives a s**t about the scene. I think he's going to do a second pressing of the EP soon, so if anyone out there didn't get it, you'll get another chance.

The N.Y./N.J. area has the biggest concentration of skinheads in the U.S. Why do you think the scene is so large there? Do the skins generally get along or are there problems between crews?
One of the reasons the scene is pretty big around here is because there are quite a few Oi and punk bands around, which results in a lot of shows happening. I don't see any problems between skins in NYC and N.J. We all go to shows and parties together and there isn't any trouble at all. Everyone knows everyone.

How are skinheads perceived by the police, media, and general public in your area?

Skinheads are perceived by the police, media, and public the same everywhere. Here it's no different, but they can all f**k off 'cause we won't give in.

Source: Hardy, Perry. "Interview with Oxblood." *Carry No Banners* (June 1994). Used by permission.

Pist'N'Broke

Who are the members of Pist'N'Broke and how long has the band been together?

The members of Pist'N'Broke are: Scotti Lyons—vocals; Ben Mancell—guitar; Jon Hill—bass; Patrick Trainor—drums; and Gabe Heiss—sax. The band has been together for one year.

Have any of you been in any bands before?

Ben and Gabe played in a Ska band called Etch-a-Sketch and they both currently play in a '77 punk band called Nadsat Nation.

You are the only Oi/skin band in the Detroit area that's not racist or fascist. Do you have a lot of support in your area? Do right-wingers ever cause you problems?

We don't have as much support in Detroit as we deserve. People don't take us as serious as they should because they're all jealous. We get more support and respect outside Detroit.

Who are some of your influences and favorite bands?

Some of our influences are AC/DC, Stiff Little Fingers, Sham 69, and the Clash. Some other bands that we like are Another Man's Poison, Serious Drinking, The Bruisers, and Cobra.

Can you tell us what some of your songs are about?

Our songs are basically about drinking and women.

What are your occupations besides the band?
Besides being in the band we are all jacks-of-all-trades and masters-of-none.

You played both the Oi/Ska festival in Atlanta and the United Front "convention" in D.C. What are your opinions on these events?
It's all a blur. We were told we were great.

How do you feel about the state of the skinhead movement in the U.S.?
Movement? What movement? All we can say is that it's probably not better or worse than anywhere else.

You are one of only a few U.S. Oi bands who don't seem to be influenced by hardcore. What is your opinion of hardcore? Does it have a place in the skinhead movement?
Actually, our rhythm section are totally into hardcore, but it really has no place in the skinhead movement. The bases of the skinhead cult were formed over 20 years ago, so who are we to say what it is except for stating true facts.

Source: Hardy, Perry. "Interview with Pist'N'Broke." *Carry No Banners* (November 1994). Used by permission.

Document 4

This excerpt from the fanzine Skinhead Times *provides a firsthand look at a skinhead musical festival in the early 1990s. Skinhead events were typically funded by active skinheads who supported the scene. Many times they lost money or were vilified by venues due to the reputation of the subculture. This festival was organized by Bohdan Zacharyj, one of the founders of United Front. Over the years, he put on countless shows and fests, and brought The Business, a British Oi! band, over in 1994 for their first of two appearances in the United States. The United Front was founded by four skinheads who served in the U.S. Army together at Fort Bragg, North Carolina. They were a diverse, nonracist crew who described themselves as leaving all politics, including SHARP, at the curb and focusing on the*

original values and roots of simply "skinhead." Before they disbanded in
1996, they had members in 47 states and 6 countries.

It didn't make the Geraldo show and MTV didn't do a special on it, but about 800 skinheads turned up in the middle of blackest Washington, D.C., for a weekend of music and partying in the largest East Coast American skinheads gathering anyone could remember. Nobody got arrested, there were no major injuries, the racially mixed audience danced to a number of multiracial bands, and stereotypes were demolished left and right. But the media weren't interested because without Nazis or mass violence, there was no story, right?

A nonracist skinhead organization run by a bunch of soldiers called United Front (UF) put on this Oi! and Ska Weekend Explosion (as it was formerly and rarely called, avoiding the dreaded "S" word when booking hall and hotel) on June 18–20.

This skinhead jamboree took place in two places, with bands playing evenings in the Wilson Center, a converted church in the Washington ghetto, and the skins packing the Parkview Inn in College Park, Maryland, the rest of the time. For $55 you got two nights in a hotel and 12 bands (music alone was $15).

The hotel staff seemed surprised to discover that they were being overrun by skinheads ("tell 'em we're all cancer patients" was a standard joke) and they refused to allow anyone in until all the rooms for the weekend were paid in full. But the hotel swimming pool played host to a very relaxed skinhead pool party on Saturday afternoon, while those who had the right footwear played football. Booze was everywhere, and there were beer parties in numerous rooms. About a third of those who attended the skinhead rally [were girls], a marked improvement over the usual tenth, according to the number of happy males.

It was very hot and humid all weekend and nearly everyone took their shirts off in the music hall, making for a spectacular tattoo exhibition. Unlike most occasions where skinheads have to watch out for attackers who've swallowed the media lies that all skinheads are Nazis, this time nobody had to worry. There were just too many skins, spreading out for a couple of blocks around the show site, mystifying the black neighborhood with their peaceful expeditions to shops and food bars. This feeling of security helped to promote the remarkable sense of relaxation which generally characterized the weekend. There were a couple of brief fights indoors and more on the street on Friday night, but there were no serious injuries. When asked what the cause of the fighting was, the usual reply was that racists were being kicked out.

Saturday's show proved much mellower, starting out with Ska rather than Oi!, and the daylong process of skins from different cities getting to know each other probably had something to do with it, but security was also much better.

Friday's show began at about 8 P.M. with The System from Portsmouth, New Hampshire, playing good, catchy Oi! riffs. They were followed by Broken Heroes (Oi! from northwest New Jersey), Warzone (fast hardcore from New York), Patriot (a hard-to-describe band from Chapel Hill, North Carolina, whose drummer Chip proposed marriage during the set—the girl accepted), and The Insteps (a Ska band from New York). Saturday started at 8 P.M., too, with the masterful Pietasters (Ska from Washington) Mephiskaphales (Ska from NYC), Oxblood (good New York Oi!), Stormwatch (Oi! from northern Delaware), Pist'N'Broke (an Oi! band with saxophones and Ska from Ann Arbor, Michigan), and finally Atlanta's resurrected Anti-Heros (excellent Oi!). The singer Mark dedicated a song "to the American media who picture us all as Nazis—they can suck my d*ck," before closing the show at 3:25 A.M. For those who missed the shows, it was all recorded for a possible album.

Musical events aside, what impressed me most was the mass friendliness—I felt I'd met 200 new friends. "Skinheads are all my brothers and I love them!" declared one skin, and this atmosphere of rejoicing in skinhead unity and brotherhood spread throughout the whole gathering. There were crews and individual skins who had traveled from all over the U.S. and Canada, and even from Ireland, to attend. Asked what skins had in common, the general answer was a working-class background, an eagerness to fight back when attacked, and a lofty ideal of mutual support. How many skinheads does it take to change a lightbulb? One to screw in the lightbulb and 20 others to back him up!

There were some White Power skins in attendance despite UF's warning that they were vastly outnumbered by antiracist and SHARP skins. Most of the skinheads showed little or no interest in politics at all.

When everyone returned to the hotel at 4:30 A.M. on Sunday, security staff had barred the way. Somebody had trashed the second floor and the management decided to keep everyone out. Maryland police arrived in 17 squad cars and persuaded the hotel that they should let people in to prevent a riot, as hundreds of furious skins jammed the lobby and hung about outside. At 5:15 A.M., they finally let everyone in, but kicked all the skins out again at 11 A.M.

Cynthia Barnes, Park View Inns front desk clerk, said that the skinheads "were very violent," but admitted that she was unaware any fighting and "didn't see any injuries." When asked what she meant by saying that the floor was" trashed," she explained that "skins had left beer cans in the hallway" and had been "skateboarding naked in the hallways." One skin, she said, had urinated in front of a window—"they didn't care who saw them." The reason the hotel's manager, Viera Safai, had barred the skins from their rooms was because they were "very drunk and loud," although she conceded that other hotel guests were not given drunkenness or decibel tests before being allowed to return to the rooms. She didn't think anyone knew in advance that it was a skinhead gathering the hotel was hosting.

According to local organizer Lisa Meetre, however, Safai knew a week in advance that this was a skinhead gathering. A second nearby hotel where rooms had been booked refused to allow skins in at all. The Parkview kicked out 14 roomfuls of individuals, Lisa said, supposedly for breaking into the pool in the middle of the night. Damage to the second floor amounted to $1,400 by the hotel's reckoning. Lisa had to pay $500 for it from her own pocket and $211 from the events funds (all of the profit). but she is contesting her legal responsibility for the rest. Not at all discouraged, Lisa wants to put on the event again next year.

Because of the trouble at the hotel and the general lack of sleep, Sunday afternoon's big skinhead rally against racism and media lies outside the White House was canceled. Too bad, because it might have made the local news—even without Nazis.

Source: Donny the Punk. "Skinheads Invade Washington. D.C." *Skinhead Times* 11 (August–October 1993): 3. Used by permission.

Document 5

The rhetoric of racist ideology is one that empowers males and defines women's role as vessels for sustaining the white race. Images of the white woman as both goddess and wife/mother are seen repeatedly in racist literature. The publication National Socialist Skinhead *references the importance of skinhead women to the Chicago scene: "These beautiful white girls are working hard to keep the holy white race alive, bringing forth children of good race, excited about getting pregnant and giving life."*[1] *Women are not expected or required to be active in the manner of men in the movement.*

Throughout the development of the skinhead subculture, many women have played key roles in the development of their scene. This is no less true in the White Power movement. Females were active in WAR Skins and other racist groups, for example. Liz Sherry was a founding member and spokesperson for Hammerskins. Some women published their own newsletters, had female-only organizations, and took active roles in planning large-scale events such as the Aryan Fest. A female member of Western Hammerskins distributed music and other merchandise under the name Totenkopf services. A male member of American Front remembers, "There were certainly skinhead girls around the White Power scene but not too many of them took a forward role in White Power activism. It was more of a masculine thing." One skinhead estimates that the status of women differed depending on the organization. As with the skinhead scene in general, a large amount of chauvinism was evident in racist skinhead groups; while many men paid lip service to the rhetoric of women being the key to the existence of the white race, in actuality women were not treated with the respect such rhetoric implied. This duality between racial ideology and feminism can be seen in the foreword written in the flagship issue of Valkyrie, *a newsletter covering racist women's issues.*

Women and the White Supremacist Movement

What has been on my mind all too often: the role of Aryan women within our resistance. It seems that our people have drastically regressed in their thought-process and actions, for now we find ourselves debating whether or not a woman should have an active role within our resistance.

For some, childbearing is the extent of their involvement (which is an obvious necessity and the greatest gift a woman can give to her race), but for others this does not satisfy their desire to advance our people. Those men who long for "seen but not heard women" desire that which evolves from an alien culture. The tribes which we derive from (i.e., Celtic, Nordic, etc.) did not produce a feeble breed of Aryan women. So why should we modify our instinctive behavior into being meek?

All Aryan women should strive to achieve what is best for the future of our race and not be restricted from thoughts or actions that are beneficial to our people's future. Those who disagree have no place in our resistance, period.

Source: Excerpt from the white supremacist women's publication, *Valkyrie*. Used by permission.

Documents 6 and 7

Like punk music, skinhead songs from the 1980s and 1990s reflected what was happening in the musicians' lives as well as emulated themes found in British music. The following are excerpts from songs by a racist band from Chicago called White American Youth (WAY) and an antiracist band from California called Headstrong.

The lead singer of WAY recalls, "I wrote the song probably in mid- to late 1990 in response to the forming of some 'anti-racist' punk and skinhead gangs in Blue Island, Illinois, where I lived in the late '80s/early '90s. It was a jab at SHARP for being posers and immature punks."

The lead singer of Headstrong remembers, "This song was written just after the first big push to recruit young kids into the Nazi skin movement out in the San Fernando Valley. Within a couple of months, there were two dozen high school kids that shaved their heads, threw on their Docs, and played 'follow the leader.' It didn't last long, though, as their "leader" got arrested for a hate crime and the group dissolved."

Go Away

S.H.A.R.P. boy p*ssies and punk freedom fighters
You're liberal scum siding with Commie liars

On the run or on the attack
You're just little kids that can't fight back

You think you're tough
You think you're brave
Keep this up and I'll put you in a grave

Scum Hanged After Racists Prevail
That's what the S.H.A.R.P. name shall entail
They wear their boots, they think they're bad.
They're just stupid punkers that are so sad.

Go away and come and f*ck with us some other day
Don't come back or you will suffer a big attack
Go on home your mommy is calling you on the f*cking telephone

Believe in God? Well he can't save you now
So you try and f*ck with us at the next show
Got 10 more people? You think we'll run?
Sorry, man. We're going to fight till we're done.

We will always win at all costs
We've never suffered a defeat or a loss
Our blood-stained boots and fists of steel
I tell you what, we're going to make a deal
You go home and play with your friends
And when the war begins we'll meet again.

Go away and come and f*ck with us some other day
Don't come back or you will suffer a big attack
Go on home your mommy is calling you on the f*cking telephone

Man, just go away.

Source: "Go Away" lyrics by Christian Picciolini. Plug Ugly Publishing (ASCAP). Copyright 1992. All rights reserved. From the album *Walk Alone* by White American Youth (Rock-O-Rama Records). Used by permission.

Mislead Youth

national socialist, right-wing lies
see the ignorance in their eyes

power-hungry bastards are now a threat
but we'll fight back, yeah you just bet
brainwashing weak-minded youth
will they ever see the truth
neo-Nazi is the trend that's in
Two-Tone power will smash and win, smash and win, smash and win

violence is the only way to get through
do it before the Nazis get you
grab your bat and stand your ground
see a Nazi's head and start to pound

racial harmony is the key
we're all brothers meant to be free
racism is a load of sh*t
any racist come by me is gonna get hit, gonna get hit, gonna get hit

Source: "Mislead Youth" lyrics by Martin Ruane. All Rights Reserved. From the album *L.A. Bootsboys '87* by Headstrong. Copyright 2007 (Disconnected Records). Used by permission.

Document 8

If there were a skinhead anthem created by an American skinhead band, the song "Crucified for Our Sins" would be it. Recorded in 1982 by Iron Cross, it was made even more popular when it was covered by Agnostic Front in 1987. Sab Grey, the lead singer of Iron Cross, says the inspiration for the song was "basically talking about how life was every day. In those days everyone had it in for us and we were only teenagers! Grown men would stop their cars to get out and punch the crap out of us. So yeah, we were fighting back!"

"Crucified for Our Sins"

They ask why do we dress this way
Live for now—Don't understand today
See the kids—But don't hear what they say
Close your eyes and look the other way

Say the end justifies the means
Gonna lock us up and throw away the keys

Crucified—Crucified for your sins
Crucified—Crucified for your sins

They don't know our feelings—only desperate cries
They see reflections through distorted eyes
We don't care because it breaks their views
Got to learn to fight to live
Before they grind us under heel

We're the targets so easy to find
And we're the ones that won't stay in line
I find myself nailed to a cross
For something that I didn't do
It's your fault you've ruined our lives
And we're the ones you crucify
You're the ones who commit the crimes
But it's always us who do the time

Source: "Crucified for Our Sins" written by Sab Grey. All rights reserved. From the EP *Skinhead Glory* by Iron Cross. Copyright, 1982. Dischord Records/Skinflint Records. Used by permission.

Document 9

To combat bias-motivated crimes, the U.S. federal government relied on the Civil Rights Act for federal prosecution. This legislation was originally designed to prosecute large organizations such as the Ku Klux Klan. Because many hate crimes were committed by individuals acting on their own, however, the states passed their own enhanced bias crime laws to address the loop holes in the federal laws. This type of legislation became the chief means of controlling the growth of racist skinheads by allowing for the prosecution of individuals unaffiliated with larger groups. Due to these laws, many skinheads convicted of criminal acts were given harsher sentences. Following is the federal statute used to prosecute racist groups as well as a hate crime statute from the state of Illinois.

Title 18, U.S.C., Section 241 Conspiracy Against Rights

This statute makes it unlawful for two or more persons to conspire to injure, oppress, threaten, or intimidate any person of any state, territory or district in the free exercise or enjoyment of any right or privilege secured to him/her by the Constitution or the laws of the United States (or because of his/her having exercised the same). It further makes it unlawful for two or more persons to go in disguise on the highway or on the premises of another with the intent to prevent or hinder his/her free exercise or enjoyment of any rights so secured. Punishment varies from a fine or imprisonment of up to ten years, or both; and if death results, or if such acts include kidnapping or an attempt to kidnap, aggravated sexual abuse or an attempt to commit aggravated sexual abuse, or an attempt to kill, shall be fined under this title or imprisoned for any term of years, or for life, or may be sentenced to death.

Source: "Conspiracy Against Rights," Title 18 *U.S. Code*, Section 241. Available at Lexis-Nexis: www.lexisnexis.com. Accessed September 10, 2011.

Current Illinois State Hate Crime Law

Chapter 720. Criminal Offenses
Criminal Code
Criminal Code of 1961
Title III. Specific Offenses
Part B. Offenses Directed against the Person
Subdivision 15. Intimidation

Sec. 12-7.1. Hate crime.

(a) A person commits a hate crime when, by reason of the actual or perceived race, color, creed, religion, ancestry, gender, sexual orientation, physical or mental disability, or national origin of another individual or group of individuals, regardless of the existence of any other motivating factor or factors, he commits assault, battery, aggravated assault, misdemeanor theft, criminal trespass to residence, misdemeanor criminal damage to property, criminal trespass to vehicle, criminal trespass to real property, mob action or disorderly conduct as these crimes are defined in Sections 12-1, 12-2, 12-3, 16-1, 19-4,

21-1, 21-2, 21-3, 25-1, and 26-1 of this Code, respectively, or harassment by telephone as defined in Section 1-1 of the Harassing and Obscene Communications Act, or harassment through electronic communications as defined in clauses (a)(2) and (a)(4) of Section 1-2 of the Harassing and Obscene Communications Act.

(b) Except as provided in subsection (b-5), hate crime is a Class 4 felony for a first offense and a Class 2 felony for a second or subsequent offense.

(b-5) Hate crime is a Class 3 felony for a first offense and a Class 2 felony for a second or subsequent offense if committed:

(1) in a church, synagogue, mosque, or other building, structure, or place used for religious worship or other religious purpose;

(2) in a cemetery, mortuary, or other facility used for the purpose of burial or memorializing the dead;

(3) in a school or other educational facility, including an administrative facility or public or private dormitory facility of or associated with the school or other educational facility;

(4) in a public park or an ethnic or religious community center;

(5) on the real property comprising any location specified in clauses (1) through (4) of this subsection (b-5); or

(6) on a public way within 1,000 feet of the real property comprising any location specified in clauses (1) through (4) of this subsection (b-5).

(b-10) Upon imposition of any sentence, the trial court shall also either order restitution paid to the victim or impose a fine up to $1,000. In addition, any order of probation or conditional discharge entered following a conviction or an adjudication of delinquency shall include a condition that the offender perform public or community service of no less than 200 hours if that service is established in the county where the offender was convicted of hate crime. The court may also impose any other condition of probation or conditional discharge under this Section.

(c) Independent of any criminal prosecution or the result thereof, any person suffering injury to his person or damage to his property as a result of hate crime may bring a civil action for damages, injunction or other appropriate relief. The court may award actual damages, including damages for emotional distress, or punitive damages. A judgment may include attorney's fees and costs. The parents or legal guardians, other than guardians appointed pursuant to the Juvenile Court Act or the Juvenile Court Act of 1987, of an unemancipated minor shall be liable for the amount of any judgment for actual damages rendered against such minor under this subsection (c) in any amount not exceeding the amount provided under Section 5 of the Parental Responsibility Law.

(d) "Sexual orientation" means heterosexuality, homosexuality, or bisexuality. (Source: P.A. 93-463, eff. 8-8-03; 93-765, eff. 7-19-04; 94-80, eff. 6-27-05.)

Source: Ill 720 ILCS 5/12-7.1 Available at Lexis-Nexis: www.lexisnexis.com. Accessed September 10, 2011.

Documents 10 and 11

One of the primary forms of recruitment for both White supremacist and antiracist skinhead factions was flyers passed out at concerts and schools. Often these flyers carried the organizers' home addresses or, if they could afford them, post office box numbers. This form of communication meant that, in some cities, finding one's rivals wasn't very difficult. The following is a flyer from the group SHARP and a letter written by racist skinheads to a California SHARP group called the Madskins. The letter was a response to a flyer distributed at a show. The group that wrote this letter mailed back the flyer with a swastika drawn on it.

Excerpt from a SHARP Flyer

Don't Crucify All Skinheads for the Actions of Just a Few
There seems to be an ongoing trend within the media which involves the reporting of the activities in the skinhead movement. Although there is truth in what the media has to say, it tends to be very one sided and incomplete. The truth of the matter is that there are quite a few factions within the movement, but (we feel) only one true SKINHEAD.

The true SKINHEAD is one who follows and tries to keep alive the original ways. This movement was *not* originally racially biased and in fact much of SKINHEAD fashion and music have been directly influenced by the West Indian Blacks known as Rude Boys or "Rudies."

We are not trying to deny the existence of so-called "SKIN-HEADS" who express and follow Nazi and white power Beliefs. What we are trying to do is establish the fact that this is not the definitive behavior of most SKINHEADS. SKINHEADS are generally hard-working patriotic men and women with respectable morals and beliefs which tend to be overlooked or ignored because of the media's interpretation of the movement. This has become a severe threat to true (non-racial) SKINHEADS, jeopardizing their health and (in some severe cases) their lives. For this reason we are asking you, the public, to become aware of the truth and realize that because of the ignorance of a few, the lives of some good, innocent people are being threatened.

White Power Letter

Dear Mad,

So Nazis are bald punks? I have been to shows and I have seen p*ssy little Two Tones get chased out by the proud white working skins. You guys are the bald punks! And the reason us White (proud White) people have been on T.V. and the radio is because we have the balls to tell our feelings. All you guys are is just a bunch of race-mixing queers! You guys have your so-called n*gger skinheads but you know there's no such thing. So traditionals watch out, cause this is proud white man's land—always has been, always will be, and we're gonna beat you n*gger lovers into the ground.

White Power

Write back to the Proud Skins (address omitted)

Document 12

This is one of the earliest academic accounts of the beginnings of the skinhead subculture in existence. This article is an adaptation of Eric Andersen's dissertation tracing the emergence of the San Francisco skinhead scene in the summer of 1985. Andersen was one of the first academics to distinguish skinheads from the punk subculture in the United States and to interview the skinheads who eventually shaped a major scene in California. Used by permission.

Skinheads by Eric Andersen: From San Francisco Hardcore Punks to Skinheads

The first hint of the skinhead subculture in San Francisco and elsewhere in the United States came in the form of a major stylistic change within punk that marked the transition between punk and hardcore punk. While punk began in the United States in the mid-1970s as a musical form (punk rock), it was among Britain's disaffected working-class young that the subculture of the punk rocker took shape as a highly creative stylistic ensemble. Punk style cohered around what Burr calls an "ordered ideology of inversion" (1985: 935). Punks presented an aesthetic negative in that what was valued by the greater society was detested and inverted. As punk began to die out in London in 1980, youths in San Francisco and Los Angeles strengthened their commitment to punk by going "hardcore."

Drawing on familiar punk themes to express their own identity, hardcore punks continued to cultivate the punk ethos that, above all, it is good to shock. Hardcore bands played a faster, angrier, and more aggressive form of punk music. In comparison to the multi-colored, often clown-like guise of the British punks, the hardcore look, with its emphasis on black thrift-shop fare, biker-style leather clothing, chains, and sharply studded wristbands, is often more foreboding. Tattooed and painted (on clothing) anarchy A's, skulls, snakes and individualized slogans like "I'm Rude, Crude, and Socially Unacceptable" abounded. Pierced noses and multiple earrings, featuring miniature skulls, daggers, and hand grenades, became commonplace. The spiked hair of early punks gave way to a variety of new hair styles, including military-style haircuts dyed jet black and platinum blonde, mohawks, and shaven heads. Along with skin haircuts, hardcore punks were quick to add full skinhead attire to their wardrobe. Skinhead fashion was appropriated because, as stated by one hardcore punk, "It was a new way to stop traffic" (British skinhead fashion as American punk *bricolage*).

By 1983 the skinhead uniform came to denote toughness and a readiness for violence. Thus the first step in the development of a skinhead group in San Francisco, aside from the initial adoption of the skinhead look by some hardcore youths, occurred when skinhead attire became an alternate form of punk apparel, chosen for being a "tough" look. This look was particularly prevalent among what skinheads and other members of San Francisco's punk subculture commonly referred to as "thug rockers." Thug rockers, also called "chaos punks," "radical punks," and "mohicans" (after their tall mohawks), were those youths within San Francisco's burgeoning hardcore scene who were most attracted to what they saw as punk's violent and nihilistic aspects and to shock value for shock value's sake. Accused by other youths of having a "punker than thou attitude" and of being "jocks who were cut from the football team," thug rockers (mostly males) tested their "hardcoreness" by trying to "out-thrash" other dancers in the "pit" (the area in front of the stage), with thrash dancing becoming increasingly more violent as contact became more frequent and turbulent. These youths were responsible for most of the "non-skinhead"–related fighting that, when I conducted my field research, occurred at approximately every other hardcore gig.

At the same time many thug rockers were beginning to dress as skinheads, a growing number of San Francisco's punks were becoming "peace punks." While the words "punk" and "anarchy" were connected as early as 1977 with the release of the Sex Pistols' punk classic, *Anarchy in the U.K.*, and the subsequent donning of the anarchy symbol by punk youths, it was the British band Crass that was the first to equate anarchy with something other than disorder, taking it out of the realm of shock and adopting it as an ideology (well exemplifying the changing nature of youth subcultural *bricolage*). Subsequently, Britain's peace punks inspired peace punk or "anarcho" divisions within, among others, San Francisco's hardcore scene. Several of San Francisco's punk bands, and their fans, adopted the anarchist/pacifist ideology and the emphasis on egalitarianism, tolerance (including being anti-racist, anti-sexist, and pro-gay rights), animal rights, vegetarianism, and living in "collectives" (squat communes) most closely associated with Crass.

By the summer of 1984, often referred to by local hardcore punks as the "summer of the peace punk," peace punks were exercising a strong influence over San Francisco's punk community. As learned from newspaper articles in San Francisco's *Examiner* (Guevarra, 1984; Rosenfeld, 1984) and *Chronicle* (Page and Shilts, 1984; Iwata and Wallace, 1984) and from interviews conducted with youths who took part in the demonstrations, San Francisco's peace punks were at their most active during the week of protests associated with the 1984 Democratic National Convention. As the convention began, anarcho punks, with other hardcore youths in tow, involved themselves in the "Democratic War Chest Tours." Claiming that the U.S. electoral system is a facade for the international corporations that fund exploitation around the world and invest in nuclear weapons, those involved in the "tours" sought to expose the Democratic Party's connection to these corporations. By week's end thousands of punks had participated and hundreds of protesters had been arrested. Moreover, around 5,000 youths, appropriately described by one hardcore punk as "More punks than I'd ever seen in one place before," turned out for a "Rock Against Reagan/Racism" concert to hear politically oriented hardcore bands such as the Dicks and Dead Kennedys, and anarcho/peace bands like M.D.C. and Reagan Youth, deliver lyrics such as "In U.S., A's for anarchy, not bullsh*t democracy, I want total liberty, I want peace and anarchy" (*U.S.A.*, Reagan Youth).

As evidenced by such large-scale punk participation, by the summer of 1984, San Francisco's peace punks had succeeded in making it "more punk" to be politically aware and active. They also made inroads into changing the image that punk style conveys to non-punks. Many punks, however, were highly critical of San Francisco's peace punks. Those who took punk to mean "thinking for yourself" accused them of being too willing to accept whatever ideological directions Britain's anarcho punks offered. Of particular importance to understanding the stylistic formation of San Francisco's skinheads, thug rockers had their own reasons for disliking peace punks. As stated by one youth:

> I got pretty disillusioned when punk went from a "f*ck the world," obnoxious attitude to politics. Also, when the peace punks started, I thought it was kind of lame. Ya know, it's O.K. to be politically aware, but it has no place in punk rock by my definition. Friends of mine were saying, "Don't be so obnoxious because no one will listen to us." Well, I'm not in punk to be respected or to be listened to.

It (politics) also took a lot of the fun and unity out of it, with shows becoming more like political forums, instead of like I'm a punk you're a punk. That plus the scene just got so big.

It was during the summer of 1984, when San Francisco's peace punks were at their most active, that some youths—many of them punk rockers already clothed in skinhead garb—began to see and refer to themselves as skinheads. This newfound separateness was expressed through skinhead-versus-punk fighting and the taking over of the pit (forcing punks out of the pit through physically intimidating thrash dancing) at hardcore shows. Occasionally, these youths would also take over the stage to shout such things as "Skinheads unite" and "Skinheads rule" into the microphone. Their desire for separateness was further stylistically expressed through an increasing interest in the history of their new subcultural identity, as evidenced in the sudden preponderance of such items as Skrewdriver T-shirts (a British white-power skinhead band funded by the National Front), SHAM '69 tattoos, Union Jack and English flag patches, and other *bricolage* of the British skinhead. At this time there were approximately 200 skinheads in San Francisco. As these youths began to comprehend the demands associated with being a *real* skinhead, their numbers dwindled. The ideology of the British skinhead with its emphasis on nationalism and racism was not shock value as usual. Some of the skinheads who looked at skinhead subcultural history and liked what they saw formed the core of the S.F. Skins.

The S.F. Skins

Who's the king, king of the skins? What's their name? The S.F. Skins. Who takes care of the king of the skins? What's their name? Bootwomen. (An S.F. Skin chant)

Young and bored and tired of the disco? Shave your head and come to San Francisco.—*Summer of Love*, the Afflicted (a local hardcore punk band's sarcastic response to the S.F. Skins)

Heads shaven and clad in red braces attached to neatly pressed jeans "sawed-off" four inches above the ankle to expose well-polished Doc

Marten boots, the S.F. Skins contrasted greatly with the hippies who once roamed the streets in the Haight-Ashbury district. They began as "drinking and fighting buddies," all males, who turned to a skinhead identity out of an increasing sense of alienation from the punk subculture. By the winter of 1985, along with some departures and additions (including the Bootwomen), these youths had become the S.F. Skins. Totaling 25 males and 9 females, ranging in ages 14 to 29, many living together in a few apartments located in the "Haight," the S.F. Skins, as I saw them in the summer of 1985, had developed into San Francisco's first unified skinhead crew.

As noted, prior to becoming skinheads most of the S.F. Skins were hardcore punks of the thug rocker variety. In presenting some of the stylistic elements and corresponding focal concerns that characterize the S.F. Skins, I hope to further explore the meaning behind this metamorphosis.

Graffiti at hardcore clubs and on the streets like "The S.F. Skins share one mind," skinhead chants such as "All for one and all on one," and complaints by punks that if "you f*ck with (provoke) one skin you are f*cking with all the skins" served as continuous reminders to those involved in San Francisco's punk scene of the importance of unity to the S.F. Skins. During my interviews with them, unity was also the most common reason given for why these youths changed subcultural affiliations. As stated by one youth:

> Hey you know what, I used to have a mohawk and I still used to fight. But then I found out that all my other buddies with mohawks and sh*t, they were too chickensh*t to fight. So I said, "F*ck this," and I shaved my head and became a skinhead. And ever since then I ain't had my ass beat. Because if a bunch of people jump on me, we're coming back twice as strong. It's called unity, man, and punk rockers ain't got no unity. They're a bunch of wimps and that's why we beat them up.

Skinhead unity involves more than the ability to rely on others for assistance in fights (as one skinhead said, "Right or wrong, skins will always back up skins"). The S.F. Skins support each other on a variety of levels. The following quote by another skin well exemplifies the extent of this support:

Unity is what it's all about. We're trying to make a family-type thing. I mean up here everyone chips in for food and for beer and stuff, and if someone isn't working, someone else covers his ass. I can leave a hundred dollars sitting in the room and no one will touch it. We share anything and everything. Cigarettes, beer, pot, food, places to sleep when someone is down and out. We're a family and we love each other and that's the whole thing.

This closeness is further expressed by the way the S.F. Skins refer to one another as "brother" and "sister," often justifying their actions, violent and otherwise, by saying that they have to "protect their little brothers/sisters" and what "they as a group believe in." For these youths, their new subcultural affiliation, particularly as it lent itself to the formation of a skinhead crew, allowed for a focus on unity and belonging that, at that time, had no punk equivalent.

As a whole, San Francisco's hardcore population had discouraged the formation of what these youths called "gang mentalities" within punk. Even in those cases where smaller close-knit alliances did form, as in the case of the "Jaks" (a group of "skate punks" who had initiation rites, spent most of their time together, and displayed their group "colors" on the backs of their jackets), these youths had not cultivated the strong sense of "we" versus "they" seen among the S.F. Skins, nor had they sought to ostracize themselves from the rest of the punk community. In this sense, while the S.F. Skins cannot be said to be trying to "magically" retrieve a sense of working-class community like their British cousins, they might be trying to retrieve the more vigorous and encompassing sense of belonging that went along with being a punk in the early days. This interpretation is supported by general comments made by some of the older S.F. Skins comparing being a skinhead today to what it was like to be a punk early on when San Francisco's punk community was smaller and more closely knit. For some of these youths, the skinhead crew may also have provided a sense of family, that as runaways, they may have never had.[2] Unity, then, can be seen as a focal concern of the S.F. Skins. By becoming skinheads the S.F. Skins were able to do more than appropriate the *bricolage* of British skinhead fashion; they were able to organize a new domain of belonging à la their British counterparts.

As with the British skinhead crew, the S.F. Skins' sense of "we" versus "they" also extended into neighborhood loyalties. In Britain, however, the emphasis on skinhead unity and territoriality arose simultaneously as two sides of the same coin, skinhead mobs being somewhat natural extensions of working-class neighborhoods. For the S.F. Skins, who have no real ties in a historical sense to the Haight-Ashbury district, territoriality appeared more as an afterthought. That it became important at all is perhaps best explained as a stylistic expression of unity and as a quest for space signifying difference. It can also be seen in terms of the S.F. Skins' apparent idealization of British skinheads, as part and parcel of a desire to do things correctly. In this sense, the importance of territory reveals another S.F. Skin focal concern—a desire to be seen as authentic. In this way it was akin to wearing British-imported Fred Perry shirts, bomber jackets, and Doc Marten boots in the *correct* British skinhead colors (respectively, white; black or green; black or "cherry red") or referring to themselves by the British terms "crew" or "mob" instead of the more American-ized term "gang." Whatever the case, while most of these youths had lived in the "Haight" only a short time, they came to see it as *their* neighborhood. The clearest declaration of their presence was the expropriation of Buena Vista Park, which became known as "Skinhead Hill."

Residents of the Haight-Ashbury district leaned toward the *San Francisco Examiner*'s assessment of the S.F. Skins' contributions to the neighborhood, well summarized by the title, "Haight Angered by Rightist Skinhead Thugs" (Ginsburg, 1985). But the skinheads saw themselves in a much more favorable light. Like British skins, in their eyes they were protecting the neighborhood from, and ridding it of, unwanted elements. Some of these "unwanted elements" are men-tioned in the following quotes by a Bootwoman and a male skin, respectively:

We're going to start holding meetings, to sit and discuss having patrols in the area. To keep the crime rate down. Sit and discuss, like, patrolling the streets to make sure that these n*ggers, cholos (Latino youths), or anyone else that don't belong in this neighborhood don't come up here and think they are going to ruin this neighborhood.

They're not. We just chased five n*ggers down the road the other night.

That's disgusting man. You've seen, ya know, those gay dudes walking around the street kissing, holding hands and sh*t. And hippies that are all over each other on the corner. That's disgusting for our street and we won't stand for it.

Although the "cleaning-up" of the neighborhood was more often talked about than engaged in, the S.F. Skins were not averse to actively backing up their statements by "sinking in the boot."[3]

The importance of violence to the group identity of the S.F. Skins cannot be overly stressed. Like the British skinhead crew members Brake (1974) interviewed, those youths who comprised the S.F. Skins were prepared to engage in violence, often referred to as *aggro* (British slang for "aggression"), at all times. As one skin said:

Everybody's got to fight. And we don't go out looking for fights but we know if we go out, the fight will appear in front of us. And it doesn't take much to get us to fight. Someone will make some stupid remark. Like the other night we were walking the streets after a show, ya know, and there's six of us. And these five guys want to make a remark. And it's like you can tell we're all lit up, we're goin' "Ya ha ha!", ya know. Because we had just gotten into a bunch of fights with a bunch of punks at the show and sh*t, because they wanted to be stupid. And it's just like they wanted to be stupid. And it's just like they wanted to say something, so they all got their asses kicked.

As "near equal" crew members, Bootwomen were in no way exempt from participating in skinhead violence. For instance, one Bootwoman described the part she and another female skin played in the above confrontation:

So the guys are doing it (fighting) and me and Mo, me and Mo are standing behind with bottles broke and we're ready to back 'em up. I mean if the dudes took off, we were going to take 'em. And that's how it is. The girls just don't have to sit there and play with themselves, ya know. Like the guys do most of the sh*t and the girls stand behind just in case they need an extra boot.

Further describing the role of Bootwomen in skinhead violence, a male skin adds:

Have you ever been in that situation where there is some smart-ass chick who comes up to a guy and starts talking all kinds of sh*t because she thinks the guy ain't going to hit her? We've got these girls here that will kill her. So therefore, therefore, not even the smart-ass little punk girls can get away with it, because they think that's all they can do.

Importantly, most of these youths stressed that they liked to fight prior to becoming skinheads. Many had already spent time in "juvie" (reform school) or in jail for violent actions. Statements such as this one are typical: "I was just as violent as I am now when I had a mohawk." Moreover, as former thug rockers (in most cases), the S.F. Skins described themselves as those punks who, unlike other hard-cores, "wouldn't put up with people badmouthing them and staring at them and sh*t." They also described themselves as being resentful of peace punks—also referred to as "new breed" punks, "p*ssy punks," and "Crassholes"—for, as one skinhead said, "trying to get a better name for themselves by being associated with peace and anti-nuclear stuff." Likewise, they complained that peace punks took punk's original violent message and turned it into a "peace and love utopia." With this in mind, it appears that in changing subcultural affiliations, the S.F. Skins had, in part, given further legitimacy, through well-established British skinhead stylistic elements, to a preexisting focal concern, their fascination with violence. At the same time, their skinhead metamorphosis allowed them to express their disdain for, and difference from, "new breed" punks.

Although most of San Francisco's hardcores recognized a variety of subgroups within the overall punk population, the S.F. Skins typically divided punks into just two types: thug rockers and peace punks. As stated by one skinhead:

They split up in two ways. The f*ckin' radical punks are the thug rockers, O.K.? Then you've got your p*ssy punks or peace punks. The peace punks are the people we don't like. They won't stand up for themselves. It's just all this, ya know, peace, peace, peace. They're just f*ckin' hippies. I mean peace is O.K. as long as it's not f*ckin' with me. If it f*ckin' walks over my line and f*ckin' disturbs me, then f*ck that sh*t. I don't want it up in my face.

Thug rockers were tolerated because "they're tough motherf*ckers" and because they "don't put America down all the time." They were also tolerated out of respect for earlier friendships. By placing the much larger "non-thug rocker" punk population into a broadened peace punk category, the S.F. Skins created an even greater sense of "we" versus "they" and enhanced their feelings of group unity in the face of a youth scene dominated by ideological rivals. Moreover, by assuming a skinhead identity, these youths inherited an established tradition of skinhead-versus-punk animosity forged first within a British setting.

Continuing the aforementioned tradition, the S.F. Skins frequented punk clubs, not only to fight, but to stylistically assert a sense of subcultural pride and superiority—a further expression of their focal concern to be seen as something very different from punks. As stated by one skinhead, "To be a skin you have to carry yourself tall and be proud." Conversely, the same youth continued, "Punks are too embarrassed by all their whining and sniveling to take pride in themselves." Likewise, whereas punks were seen by skinheads as being "slobs," skinhead pride was shown in meticulously kept skinhead attire. As stated by one Bootwoman, "You'll never see a dirty skin. Try to find one. You can't." On the streets their heads were always held high. At clubs, they walked, with upper body taut, through any group of punks who got in their way. If a hardcore youth pushed back or made a comment, a fight was likely to break out. If another punk joined in or tried to break up the fight, he became the collective target of those skinheads present and was beaten up (often severely) for interrupting "skin business." Occasionally, skinheads would punch punks at random, without warning or provocation. The skin would then wait for the punk to strike back. If there was no response, the skin had won yet another fight against a punk rival. Assaults typically went unanswered because as one punk put it, "Even if you win, you lose." Skinhead-versus-punk altercations also occurred

on the dance floor. In what is one of the more obvious stylistic and ritu-
alistic expressions of difference, while hardcore punks thrashed in the
standard counterclockwise fashion, the S.F. Skins would often start cir-
cling in the opposite direction. At this point, thrash dancing, an already
physically intimidating act, would turn into what the skins called "a
game of king of the pit."

While the S.F. Skins were of mixed socioeconomic backgrounds,
in assuming a skinhead identity, and in idealizing British skins, these
youths came to define themselves as champions of the working class
(giving further expression to the focal concern of authenticity). In so
doing they adopted a number of *perceived* working-class and/or British
skinhead values, including a strong work ethic. As stated by one youth:

> We all work. And we're all working-class people. And we ain't f*ckin'
> bums. We don't squat. Most of us are construction workers. Terri,
> though, he's a (house) painter.

Work, in fact, completed the cycle of skinhead recruitment. Suc-
cessful recruitment required a youth to show that he/she would not
"cut and run" during fights, especially when fighting alongside other
skins. It also required having one's head shaved in an informal initiation.
Nonetheless, a youth was not considered a full member until he/she
stopped wearing one of the extra pairs of "house boots" (a pair of older
Doc Marten boots previously owned by another S.F. Skin), purchasing
their own pair of boots with money earned from employment.

While work played an important role in their subcultural identity,
with the exception of some of the Bootwomen who were free to
engage in "non-masculine" work in restaurants, none of these youths
were employed on a full-time basis. Most skins worked only occasionally as part-time physical laborers. The S.F. Skins placed most of the
blame for their inability to secure full-time employment on "foreign-
ers." As stated by one skin, the problem is that "Lady Liberty just
keeps spreading her legs to let all the scum in." Another youth added,
"We gotta start thinkin' about Americans for a change or we're gonna
have to fight Mexicans, Chinks, and Pakis and sh*t just to get jobs at
McDonald's." The S.F. Skins were also in favor of doing away with
public assistance and social service programs. This attitude is seen in
the following quote by a skinhead youth that also expresses how the

S.F. Skins felt about African Americans, who were seen as taking "white jobs":

> They should be back in Africa man, you know, fighting Apartheid or whatever. They should be over there because all they do is start trouble. They go around mugging people and raping people and sh*t. S*ck off the government. F*cking go on welfare and take everybody's taxes.

By adopting a strong work ethic the S.F. Skins also further defined themselves in opposition to punks, who were seen as "lazy asses" and as "bums." Punks were continuously criticized for "begging change" and for squatting, although as former punks most of the S.F. Skins had previously engaged in these activities. The S.F. Skins were even more critical of those few youths left on San Francisco's hardcore scene who dressed like skinheads but were not S.F. Skins. Most often referred to as "street skins," the S.F. Skins accused these youths of tainting the skinhead image and described them as harshly as possible. As stated by one skin:

> Street skins ain't sh*t. They're a bunch of commie, anarchist, f*ggot, bum motherf*ckers that live under the street. They panhandle, they sleep in the f*ckin' gutter, and we don't allow them to come around here. We don't allow any panhandling up here. F*ck it man, we don't need that sh*t. I wish I saw a f*ckin' street skin panhandling on our street.

Aside from smoking marijuana, which they did not view as a real drug, the S.F. Skins took an "anti-drug abuse/pro-beer drinking" stance in support of their image of themselves as "working-class, clean-cut, all Americans." As one youth said:

> We don't do drugs; we smoke pot, but we don't do drugs. We drink Bud (Budweiser) and we hang the flag. We're American and don't every good American do the same thing?

Another youth provided further insight into the S.F. Skins' aversion to hard drugs by stating:

Hopefully we'll all die fighting in the streets and no other way. 'Cuz if you die fighting, you die the way you want to die. If you die in some wasted drug scene, then that bums you out. We've got friends (mostly thug rockers) who are doing drugs and they get all strung out and it's not worth that. It's like "Come on over, man; we will buy you beer and food and you can get off the stuff. Totally get off the speed or the heroin or whatever, get off it, ya know?" I mean I don't do drugs like that anymore and I used to.

Beer consumption also undoubtedly helped these youths live up to the demands of their fight-oriented subcultural role by helping release their inhibitions and aggressive behavior. As stated by one youth, and as frequently observed firsthand, "Usually someone has to f*ck with us first, but when we're really drunk; well, we don't always wait for stupid remarks before we go off on (punch) somebody."

As *true* skinheads and self-proclaimed members of the working class, the S.F. Skins were also quite vocal about their "anti-homosexual" sentiments and chauvinistic attitudes. During conversations and interviews, regardless of the topic at hand, these youths would frequently interject statements such as "I've got one thing to say, I hate f*ggots." And while unlike their British predecessors, the S.F. Skins had not turned "queer-bashing" into a ritualized activity, they seldom missed an opportunity for verbal harassment, which would occasionally lead to a fight.

In sharp contrast to the descriptions of the role of "skinhead girls" and the way in which they were treated in Britain (Clarke 1976a; Cohen and Roberts, 1978; Daniel and McGuire, 1972), the Boot-women were typically viewed and treated as respected equals by their male counterparts.[4] Nonetheless, the Bootwomen often described their subcultural role as secondary to that of their male counterparts, mostly because they felt they were the physically weaker sex in a violent subculture. Those female punks who occasionally dated the S.F. Skins bore the brunt of skinhead chauvinism. Male skins would also physically and verbally harass female punks at hardcore shows, e.g., "goosing them" and telling them to "get out of the pit and go back to the kitchen where you belong." The Bootwomen would often abet the chauvinism of their male counterparts, viewing most female punks as "bimbos," thereby further bolstering their perceptions of skinhead subcultural superiority. While relationships with female punks were temporary and sexual in nature, relationships between male skins and Bootwomen were more permanent and emotionally bonding. The complexity of skinhead chauvinism is illustrated in the following description of a female skin catching her skin boyfriend kissing a female punk at a party:

> They (the male skins) go at the punk bimbos and stuff like that. I caught him (her boyfriend) at a party the other night. He was kissing one girl and getting ready to kiss another girl and I said, "Goodnight, Shawny." He got busted (found out). I said, like "Who are those bimbos there?" As soon as I showed up he dropped the f*ckin' b*tch on the floor and came home with me. I just looked at her like "Well, you're just sh*t. You're lucky I don't hit you just for the hell of it."

The S.F. Skins' search for a working-class identity and authenticity is also stylistically evident in a musical context. SHAM '69, for instance, was particularly admired, not only because they were championed by British skins, but because "They were one of the first working-class bands in England." Subsequent British bands playing a skinhead variant of punk music known as "Oi" (working-class Cockney for "Hey, you"), like the Angelic Upstarts, were similarly admired because they were seen as supporting the interests and the idealized values of the working class. The S.F. Skins further valued Oi bands for "standing up for their country," but the bottom line for most of these youths was that "American hardcore rules. We have our own bands and we stand up for our own country. I'm for them." This last quote reveals yet another focal concern of the S.F. Skins: the desire to be seen not only as skinheads but as *American* skinheads. Through the activity of stylization, the S.F. Skins were able to give form to this desire.

Inspired by British skinhead involvement in the far right National Front and British Movement, the S.F. Skins introduced the ideological elements of their own "American Front" in a flier posted primarily in and around the Haight district. Addressed to "Punks, Communists, Anarchists, Hippys [*sic*], Homosexuals and other enemies of America and the American way of life," the American Front flier declared:

We the SKINHEADS will not tolerate your spreading of unwanted diseases both mental and physical. We are jailed because we use every method at our disposal to protect the decent people of this country from your unAmerican, subversive, left wing mind poison. So beware enemy's [*sic*] of the flag, Your Days Are Numbered.

The kicking-in of the Anarchist Bookstore window on Haight Street on the day that this flier was posted gave credence to the S.F. Skins' stated intentions.[5]

Whereas British skinheads had their brand of fascism largely defined for them by the National Front and the British Movement, the S.F. Skins, at this time, had no such direct political apprenticeship. In the absence of a matrix of well-established domestic fascism, the S.F. Skins transformed the ideological *bricolage* of British skinhead racist nationalism into more of an "Americanized" racist patriotism by turning to Ronald Reagan and creating "Republicanism" (my term, denoting a fascist appropriation of perceived Republican Party values). At hardcore shows and in the streets, the S.F. Skins could often be found chanting such things as "U.S.A., U.S.A.," "We're proud Republicans, proud to be Americans," "Ronald Reagan, he's my man; if he can't do it, no one can," and "Heil, Reagan; Heil, Reagan" (complete with extended arm salutes). The S.F. Skins admired Reagan for reasons such as the following:

He likes war. . . . Hey man, he ain't no chickensh*t punk rocker, like f*ckin' Carter. That f*cker lets hostages sit over there [referring to the Iranian-held hostages at the U.S. embassy in Tehran] a hundred days, man. Reagan gets out there and goes, "Yeah, f*ck that man, you let 'em go or you're dead, too, ya know."

Why are we gonna let these little countries think they're gonna push us around? That's bullsh*t, man. That's what Ron is saying. Are we gonna stand and fight or are we gonna run and fight like the hippies did in Vietnam?

These youths often spoke of making Ronald Reagan "leader for life" and of their willingness to die for him, even sending a picture of themselves along with a letter stating their intentions addressed to the White House.

"Republicanism," especially in the form of an aggressive patriotism, was a salient stylistic element within the daily lives of the S.F. Skins. When I would visit one of the skin apartments, I was invited to sit in "Archie's chair," the "chair of respect." For these youths, the television character Archie Bunker was America personified, a perceived paradigm of American working-class virtues. Other skinhead cultural heroes included General George Patton, John Wayne, and the western novelist Louis L'Amour. American flags filled the walls of skinhead apartments and flags displayed outside were carefully removed each evening. American flags also appeared as tattoos, on caps, jackets, and T-shirts, along with slogans such as "America, love it or get the f*ck out." For the Bootwomen, this stylized fetish of nationalism also appeared in red, white, and blue socks and braces. Budweiser was the beer of choice because "It's so true, Bud's so red, white, and blue." As guardians of the flag, the S.F. Skins assaulted those individuals deemed "un-American." For instance, one youth was attacked for wearing an upside-down flag on his jacket.

However, the S.F. Skins themselves commonly displayed the icons of Nazism alongside American symbols. Tattooed images of swastikas, iron crosses, saluting Hitler youth, and the flag of the Third Reich appeared alongside tattoos of Old Glory and the American eagle. The S.F. Skins were expressing a fascistic and racist sense of patriotism. As one skin said, "I'm not only a Republican, but I'm a fascist asshole son of a b*tch. I'm pulling for my race, definitely."

Racism formed another major axis of skinhead "Republicanism." Before the group formation of the S.F. Skins, some of San Francisco's skinheads were African American and Mexican American. But as an S.F. Skin:

> You believe in America, you believe in the white revolution and you believe in the existing governmental system ... If you forget everything else, just remember two things: we're white and American and proud of it.

S.F. Skins' racism seems a crystallization and legitimization of preexistent racist and anti-Semitic attitudes. For instance, one youth frequently bragged about fighting "n*ggers" and "chollos" in "juvie," and others talked about beating up "chollos" in San Francisco's Mission district as thug rockers. Another skin complained about the greed of his former Jewish employer. A skinhead identity seemed incendiary to such inchoate racism. The S.F. Skins celebrated their racism and anti-Semitism by composing and singing songs such as "N*gger, n*gger, now you gotta go now. I hate commies and I hate Jews and when I see a n*gger I want to give him the boot" (sung to the tune of *Louie, Louie*) and "I'm dreaming of a white Christmas, one without n*ggers" (sung to the tune of *White Christmas*).

Although the S.F. Skins turned out to thrash to almost any hardcore band, even to bands criticized as too leftist, anarchist, etc., they sought out and were especially fond of those few hardcore bands that reflected their own focal concerns. The entire skinhead crew typically attended any show where the F*ck Ups performed, emphatically demanding that the band play *White Boy* (a song about being white in the predominantly Latin Mission district).

> White boy in the Mission. White boy walkin' around, nobody gonna put you down, white boy. White boy, can't you see you're a minority, white boy. White boy, have some pride. White boy kill and white boy fight. White boy havin' fun, white boy buy a gun.

The skins were particularly fond of the patriotic New York hardcore band Agnostic Front. Known for songs such as *Public Assistance (No Need for)*, this band opened its San Francisco debut performance by kissing the American flag.

Finally, the "Republicanism" of the S.F. Skins allowed these youths to react in ever increasing opposition to their peace punk rivals. One youth articulated this ideological antagonism as follows:

> We got to learn what's right and what's wrong. And we have to stand, we have to stand up for it. 'Cuz these peace punks, they want to stand for anarchy and that doesn't work, you know? Anarchy cannot exist; it cannot work in this country. Because if anarchy did exist on the street today, how many people would be on the streets today? If it wasn't for the cops, a lot of people would be dead, there would be a riot.

The S.F. Skins even developed a quasi-police function vis-à-vis peace punk activities by engaging in such actions as pulling down the peace punks' anti-apartheid banners during a demonstration at the Hall of Justice. The police function of the S.F. Skins was still more evident at the No Business as Usual Day demonstration in April 1985. No Business as Usual Day was the first major protest characterized by extensive peace punk participation since the multiple arrests that ended the last day of the war tour demonstrations in the summer of 1984. In the midst of the confusion of this constantly moving street demonstration intended to disrupt "business as usual" in the Financial District, the S.F. Skins violently clashed with the mostly pacifistic peace punks. In response to an inquiry from me concerning their involvement in this demonstration, a Bootwoman responded, "That's commie. That's like f*ckin' full communist right there. We didn't walk with 'em. We walked on 'em."

Conclusion

The primary purpose of this essay was to provide some insight into the creative emergence of one of the first skinhead crews to take form in the United States. To do so adequately, it was necessary to trace the stylistic development of the S.F. Skins from Britain to San Francisco via punk rock. It was largely through appropriating from the "field of possibles" of British skins that the majority of S.F. Skins, as former thug rockers, underwent a series of dramatic transformations and were able to respond to peace punk–inspired stylistic changes within San Francisco's punk community. As stated by one youth, "When I was a thug rocker, I didn't believe in anything." In looking to their British predecessors, partly in a search for authenticity, politically dormant thug rockers who were of the opinion that punk and politics should not mix invented their own fascistic ideology. Other appropriations of the stylistic elements of British skinheads included the sudden realization of the importance of neighborhood and a kinship with the working class.

By becoming skinheads, members of the S.F. Skins were able to react in opposition to new stylistic directions developing within punk. Not wanting to be associated with pacifism, leftist political stances, and anarchy as something other than a symbol of disorder, these youths, many of them already clothed in the skinhead uniform, looked to British skinheads as a stylistic alternative. Their new identity allowed them to pursue a rigorous sense of unity forged and rationalized in relation to their peace punk rivals. By placing nearly all punks in the much despised "peace punk/p*ssy punk" category and separating themselves from them by walking tall, dressing fastidiously, working, and proudly paying rent and by confronting punks violently in and out of the pit, etc., the S.F. Skins erected numerous insulating barriers between themselves and the punk subculture. Skinhead style allowed them to stand against the peace punk subversion of the stylistic elements that first drew them to punk, while skinhead "Republicanism" served as an oppositionary complement to the activism of anarcho-peace punks. In this respect, the S.F. Skins mirrored their British predecessors, who rationalized their own stylistic formation first in relation to mods and hippies and later in relation to punks.

At first glance it might appear that in adopting a skinhead identity members of the S.F. Skins had come full circle. As former thug rockers, these youths were originally drawn to punk's "ideology of inversion." With stylistic elements cohering around the interrelated imagery of vulgarity, chaos, sexual perversion, death, violence, loathsomeness, etc., San Francisco's punks expressed their disillusionment with U.S. society by mocking it in exaggerated style. In developing a skinhead identity these youths moved from "America sucks" to "America rules," exhibiting their commitment to the U.S. and to the skinhead subculture in the form of tattooed Doc Marten boots colored red, white, and blue. Alongside tattoos indicating their commitment to the skinhead way of life, however, remained such extreme signs of a thug rocker past as tattooed aborted fetuses running up the arm of one youth and a bullet entry wound tattooed on the side of the head of another. Moreover, in an atmosphere of racial egalitarianism, tolerance, and pacifism promoted by peace punks, it was the skinhead's racist, anti-homosexual, chauvinistic, violent, and nationalistic messages that remained shocking, and in this way true to punk's original message.

As *bricoleurs* the S.F. Skins, through the activity of stylization, gave creative form to their notions of what it means to be a U.S. skinhead, drawing connections between the attire, activities, and ideology of British skins and symbols of American pride from a U.S. "field of possibles" including American flags, "America's beer" (Budweiser), conservative icons (John Wayne, Archie Bunker), and a "radicalized" version of a popular conservative president (who was, importantly, particularly despised by peace punks).[6] It was also through stylization that that these youths were able to give voice to preexisting and emerging focal concerns such as unity, violence, authenticity, and their desire to stand in opposition to their peace punk rivals.

Lastly, I do not want to leave the impression that by adopting a skinhead identity, members of the S.F. Skins *became* violent, racist, sexist, anti-gay, etc. As thug rockers, members of the S.F. Skins already had found a means of expressing their violent tendencies.[7] As skinheads, however, the S.F. Skins were able to use the medium of violence as a means of expressing their self-esteem, collective group image, and significance, within a new and seemingly more appropriate subcultural context. By becoming skinheads these youths increased the number of targets they had to choose from while providing ideological justification for their violence. Likewise, a skinhead identity allowed these youths to creatively express preexisting prejudices in a supportive environment. It was through defining themselves subculturally, however, that these youths were able to give more concrete form to what were more inchoate, less organized notions about the world.

Bibliography

Anti-Defamation League. (1993). *Young Nazi killers: The rising skinhead danger.* New York.

Brake, M. (1974). The skinheads: An English working class subculture. *Youth and Society*, 6(2), 179–199.

Brake, M. (1985). *Comparative youth culture: The sociology of youth cultures and youth subcultures in America, Britain and Canada.* London: Routledge and Kegan Paul.

Burr, A. (1985). The ideologies of despair: A symbolic interpretation of punks and skinheads usage of barbiturates. *Social Science and Medicine*, 19(9), 929–938.

Clarke, J., Hall, S., Jefferson, T., & Roberts, B. (1976). Subcultures, cultures and class. In S. Hall & T. Jefferson, (Eds.), *Resistance through rituals.* London: Hutchinson.

Clarke, J. (1976a). Style. In S. Hall & T. Jefferson, (Eds.), *Resistance through rituals.* London: Hutchinson.

Clarke, J. (1976b). The skinheads and the magical recovery of community. In S. Hall & T. Jefferson, (Eds.), *Resistance through rituals.* London: Hutchinson.

Clarke, J., & Jefferson, T. (1976). Working class youth cultures. In G. Mungham & G. Pearson, (Eds.), *Working class youth culture.* London: Routledge and Kegan Paul.

Cohen, P. (1972). Subcultural conflict and the working class community. *Working Papers in Cultural Studies 2*. Birmingham: CCCS.

Cohen, P., & Robins, D. (1978). *Knuckle sandwich: Growing up in a working-class city*. Harmondsworth: Penguin.

Coplon, J. (1988). Skinhead nation. *Rolling Stone*, December, 54–65.

Daniel, S., & McGuire, P. (1972). *The paint house: Words from an East End gang*. Harmondsworth: Penguin.

Dunning, E., Murphy, P., & Williams. J. (1986). The rise of the English soccer hooligan. *Youth and Society*, 17(4), 362–373.

Frith, S. (1983). *Sound effects: Youth, leisure and the politics of rock*. Great Britain: Constable and Company.

Ginsburg, M. (1985). Haight angered by rightist skinhead thugs. *San Francisco Examiner*. April 11, A1.

Guevarra, L. (1984). Eight arrested during anti-Falwell march. *San Francisco Examiner*. July 13.

Hamm, M. S. (1993). *American skinheads: The criminology and control of hate crime*. Westport, CT: Praeger.

Hebdige, D. (1979). *Subculture: The meaning of style*. New York: Methuen and Co.

Iwata, E., & Wallace. B. (1984). Hundreds arrested in two S.F. demonstrations. *San Francisco Chronicle*. July 20.

Levi-Strauss, C. (1972). *The savage mind*. London: Weidenfeld and Nicolson.

Miller, W. B. (1958). Lower class culture as a generating milieu of gang delinquency. *Journal of Social Issues*, 14(2), 5–19.

Moore, J. B. (1993). *Skinheads shaved for battle: A cultural history of American skinheads*. Bowling Green: Bowling Green State University Popular Press.

Page, P., &. Shilts, R. (1984). "Punk rocker protest—84 arrests," *San Francisco Chronicle*. July 17.

Ridgeway, J. (1995). *Blood in the face: The Ku Klux Klan, Aryan Nations, Nazi skinheads, and the rise of a new white culture*. New York: Thunder's Mouth Press.

Rosenfeld, S. (1984). Peace punks' week of rallies. *San Francisco Examiner*. July 21.

Taylor, I., & Wall, D. (1976). Beyond the skinheads: Comments on the emergence and significance of the glamrock cult. In G. Mungham & G. Pearson, (Eds.). *Working class youth culture*. London: Routledge and Kegan Paul.

Thompson, P. (1979). Youth culture and youth politics in Britain. *Radical America*, 13(2), 53–65.

Notes

1. *Chicago Reader* article.
2. This search for family involved one of the skinhead couples petitioning for legal guardianship of the youngest S.F. Skin, a 14-year-old runaway.
3. During my last few weeks of fieldwork the S.F. Skins were visited by members of the Hell's Angels, who own properties in the Haight-Ashbury district. While originally flattered by the attention paid to them by such "tough motherf*ckers," the Hell's Angels' warning to the skinheads to "cool it or else" undoubtedly played a role in the soon thereafter disintegration of the S.F. Skins.

4. In accordance with their "near equal" position within the crew, most of the Boot-women dressed in full male skinhead attire. A few "feminized" their appearance by wearing their hair in the style of British female skinheads (short on top with long bangs and a somewhat longer length on the sides).

5. Most members of the S.F. Skins went their separate ways shortly after the summer of 1985. The youth who authored the American Front flier founded the American Front skinhead group featured in an article in *Rolling Stone* magazine (Coplon 1988: 54–65).

6. While the S.F. Skins framed themselves within an "imagined" working class, in many ways they were stylistically reproducing American middle-class categories such as a work ethic, heterosexuality, and patriotism, albeit in an exaggerated fashion. Even their apparent "consumption" of British style could be viewed within an American middle-class framework.

7. The violent tendencies of members of the S.F. Skins are probably best explored in the context of the level of violence many of these youths experienced within their home environments.

Annotated Bibliography

Essential Print Resources

Allen, Jennifer. "Young, White, and Surrounded." *Rolling Stone* 685 (June 1994): 54.
  Focuses on Christopher David Fisher, the leader of the Fourth Reich Skins, who was on trial for conspiracy to manufacture and use destructive devices.

Blauner, Peter. "Hardcore Kids: Rebellion in the Age of Reagan." *New York* 19 (May 1986): 38–46.
  This scholarly article was one of the first accounts of the New York hardcore scene. The author was probably better known for his appearance with many of the NYHC members who became infamous on the *Phil Donahue Show,* which provided the first national exposure most Americans had to skinheads.

Blee, Kathleen. *Inside Organized Racism: Women in the Hate Movement.* Berkeley: University of California Press, 2002.
  This book details women's roles in various White Power organizations and groups. The author interviewed eight White Power skinhead women and included their observations throughout the book.

Blush, Steven. *American Hardcore: A Tribal History.* Los Angeles: Feral House, 2001.
  A book that details the history of punk across the United States. Divided by region, the sections examine many of the music movements from the 1970s until 1985.

Borgeson, Kevin. "Culture and Identity among Skinhead Women." *Michigan Socio-logical Review* 17 (2003): 99–118.
This scholarly article relies on interviews and observations to see whether what self-identified skins speak about resembles the sort of structure and thematic emphasis revealed by previous social science research.

Brake, Mike. "The Skinheads: An English Working Class Subculture." *Youth & Society* 6 (1974): 179–200.
One of the first research articles to investigate skinheads in England. It is considered one of the seminal articles on the subculture and the first one to document the actions and motivations of British skinheads.

"Britain: The Skinheads." *Time* 95, no. 23 (June 1970): 38.
One of the few American accounts of the first wave of the skinhead subculture. This article details the dress, musical tastes, and attitudes of early British skinhead youth.

Cohn, Nik. "Pop: England's New Teen Style Is Violence: England's New, Violent Teen Style." *New York Times* (March 29, 1970): 99.
The second article published in *The New York Times* about the skinhead subculture in England. It outlines the habits, music, dress, and anti-immigrant stance of the subculture. Of particular note is the author's examination of skinheads listening to Jamaican reggae, yet engaging in "Paki bashing" and racism.

Coplon, Jeff. "Skinhead Nation." *Rolling Stone* 540 (December 1988): 54–65.
Examines the rapid emergence of Nazi skinheads, the fastest-growing segment of the racist right. It includes interviews with Bob Heick, national chairman of the American Front, and Tom Metzger, head of the White Aryan Resistance (WAR). It also looks at reasons for growth of the skinhead nation.

Daniel, Susie. *The Paint House: Words from an East End Gang.* Harmondsworth: Penguin, 1972.
This book is the best primary source documenting the roots of the skinhead subculture in England. Anthropologists interviewed skinheads over a period of time and documented their daily lives, thoughts, and actions. The researchers were studying a youth gang and unwittingly documented one of the earlier skinhead crews of the time.

De Grazia, Don. *American Skin.* New York: Scribner Paperback Fiction, 2000.
A fictional account of prominent skinheads in Chicago. De Grazia was a bouncer at a popular punk venue, and he wrote stories based on the tales he heard from others in the skinhead and punk scene. The story centers on Alex Verdi, a young man who joins a multiracial group of anti-Nazi skinheads and embarks on an odyssey that takes him to the streets and eventually to prison.

Emerson, Gloria. "British Youth's Latest Turn: The Skinhead." *New York Times* (December 16, 1969): 12.

The first American news story about the skinhead subculture. The author interviewed a young skinhead in London and reported on the major aspects of the subculture as it existed in 1969. Of note is the lack of racist rhetoric and the focus on fighting motorcycle gangs as the enemy of skinheads.

Ezekiel, Raphael S. *The Racist Mind: Portraits of American Neo-Nazis and Klansmen.* New York: Viking, 1995.
This book provides detailed biographical portraits of major figures in the U.S. white supremacist movement, including John Metzger and Richard Butler, who had the most interaction with skinheads. This book includes interviews with both leaders and followers of racist movements.

Futrell, Robert, Pete Simi, and Simon Gottschalk. "Understanding Music in Movements: The White Power Music Scene." *Sociological Quarterly* 47 (2006): 275–304.
Relying on an analysis of ethnographic and documentary data, this article explains how U.S. White Power movement (WPM) activists use music to produce collective occasions and experiences that we conceptualize as the movement's music scene.

"Geraldo Rivera's Nose Broken in Scuffle on His Talk Show." *New York Times* (November 4, 1988): B3.
Geraldo Rivera's nose was broken and his face cut during a skirmish yesterday midway through the taping of a program entitled "Teen Hatemongers" on his television talk show. This was the pinnacle of skinhead notoriety in the mainstream press.

Grey, Sab. *Skinhead Army.* United States: Skinflint Press, 2007.
A novel about skinheads in the 1980s, written by Sab Grey, lead singer of the first skinhead band in the United States. His conflicted working-class protagonist Grey fights Nazis and indulges in his love of history, music, women and booze. Filled with exhilarating action and the author's unique insight into skinhead/punk culture, Grey's *Skinhead Army* provides piercing insight into the skinhead lifestyle.

Gunderson, Chris. "Anti-Racist Skinheads Ready to Strike Back at Neo-Nazis." *Utne Reader* 33 (1989): 88.
Focuses on the founding of the Syndicate, a national skinhead coalition determined to combat racist violence in the United States. The article describes the origins of the organized antiracist groups as well as the rough style of street politics resulting from the concealed rage among working-class youth.

Hackett, George, and Pamela Abramson. "Skinheads on the Rampage." *Newsweek* 110 (September 1987): 22.
One of the first mainstream articles to examine the growth of skinhead across Chicago, Dallas, Orlando, and other cities in the United States.

Hauptfuhrer, Fred, and Terry Smith. "With Ready Fists and Rage, Britain's Skinheads Alarm an Already Troubled Country." *People* 16 (September 1981): 53–54.

This article recounts the role skinheads played in the riots in London that began July 3 after a show featuring the bands the 4skins, Business, and Last Resort was prematurely shut down. It also includes interviews with various skinheads and examines the rising tide of anti-immigrant sentiment among the subculture.

Healy, Murray. *Gay Skins: Class, Masculinity and Queer Appropriation*. London: Cassell, 1996.
Examines the adoption of the skinhead look by gay men in England. Healy first traces the history of the subculture and the roles that gay skinheads played as early as the first generation of skinheads in 1969. He then chronicles the use of the skinhead imagery in the larger gay community into the 1990s.

Hebdige, Dick. *Subculture: The Meaning of Style*. New York: Methuen, 1979.
A seminal work that examines a variety of youth subcultures, especially the impact of fashion and music on these groups. In addition to skinheads, this book examines teddy boys, rockers, rudeboys, punks, and mods.

"Inside Skinhead." *Utne Reader* (July/August 1998): 38–40.
Presents an interview with Thomas Leyden, who spent a number of years in the skinhead movement before renouncing racism and going to work as a consultant for the Simon Wiesenthal Center, a human rights organization in California.

Jackson, David S. "Skinhead against Skinhead." *Time* 142 (August 1993): 42.
Examines Portland, Oregon's rival gangs of skinheads, many of whom arrived in the wake of the 1988 murder by the East Side White Pride gang of an Ethiopian student, Mulugeta Seraw.

Johnson, Garry. 1980. *The Story of Oi: A View from the Dead-end of the Street*. Manchester, England: Babylon Books.
This book was an examination of Oi! music which was popular among skinheads. It includes profiles of notable skinhead bands and song lyrics.

Knight, Nick. *Skinhead*. London: Omnibus, 1982.
One of the most influential and widely read books about skinheads ever written. It contains photos and drawings of skinheads as well as an overview of the first and second waves of skinheads in England.

Langer, Elinor. *A Hundred Little Hitlers: The Death of a Black Man, the Trial of a White Racist, and the Rise of the Neo-Nazi Movement in America*. New York: Metropolitan Books, 2003.
This book details the events leading up to, and following, the murder of Mulugeta Seraw in Portland, Oregon. It gives a good history of the WAR Skins, the Portland skinhead scene, and the aftermath of the crime. It includes biographical sketches of Dave Mazella, Ken Mieske, and other individuals involved in the murder.

Leo, John. "A Chilling Wave of Racism." *Time* 131 (January 1988): 57.
An article attributing a wave of racist incidents to skinheads, loosely organized groups of violent youths, who were perceived as emerging as the "kiddie corps" of the neo-Nazi movement. Membership nationally was estimated at 1,000 and growing.

Marshall, George. *Skinhead Nation*. Dunoon: S.T. Publishing, 1997.
The second title published by Skinhead Times (S.T.) Publishing. This collection of interviews and narratives focuses on various scenes around the world, including the United States.

Marshall, George. *Spirit of '69: A Skinhead Bible*. 2nd ed. Dunoon, Scotland: S.T. Publishing, 1994.
This book, which was originally published in 1991, was written by George Marshall, who was active in the skinhead subculture and the creator of a popular fanzine entitled *Skinhead Times*. It is widely recognized as the first book to present a balanced view of the entire skinhead subculture from its inception to the early 1990s. It includes references to skinheads in the United Kingdom, Europe, Australia, and the United States.

Maynard, Meleah. "Brothers in Arms." *City Pages* 12 (January 1990): 6.
A feature article that appeared in 1990 detailing the skinhead scene in Minneapolis. It featured interviews with the skinhead crew called the Baldies and was one of the few cover stories that featured nonracist skinheads.

Palmer, Robert. "The Pop Life: From British Racial Strife, Rock." *New York Times* (April 15, 1981): C24.
A review of the film *Dance Craze* and the context surrounding the 2Tone movement in England. For many skinheads, this film marked their first introduction to the 2Tone phenomenon that played a role in the second generation of British skinheads in the late 1970s

"The Roots of Skinhead Violence: Dim Economic Prospects for Young Men." *Utne Reader* (May/June 1989): 84.
Presents an excerpt from an article published in the November 1987 issue of *Dollars & Sense* about the roots of skinhead violence in the United States. According the article, declining economic conditions were affecting young white males and driving them toward violence.

Sarabia, Daniel, and Thomas E. Shriver. "Maintaining Collective Identity in a Hostile Environment: Confronting Negative Public Perception and Factional Divisions within the Skinhead Subculture." *Sociological Spectrum* 24 (2004): 267–294.
This research article employs both primary and secondary sources to examine collective identity among traditional skinheads who are not racist. The results illustrate that skinhead groups are diverse. The findings indicate that traditional skinhead factions see racism as an abomination of original skinhead culture, and as a result, many groups have taken action to confront their racist skinhead counterparts.

Savage, Jon, and Nick James. "New Boots and Rants." *Sight & Sound* 17, no. 5 (2007): 38–42.
The article discusses Great Britain's youth culture of the early 1980s as it relates to the motion picture *This Is England*. The film, from director Shane Meadows, concerns a young English boy who is recruited into skinhead culture. The article discusses the influence of punk rock on British culture, and the discontent felt by

many young Britons of the early 1980s during the administration headed by British Prime Minister Margaret Thatcher.

Simi, Pete. "Hate Groups or Street Gangs? The Emergence of Racist Skinheads." In James F. Short and Lorine A. Hughes, eds. *Studying Youth Gangs*. Lanham, MD: AltaMira Press, 2006, pp. 145–160.
This chapter is based upon the author's dissertation. He centers his research on interviews with skinhead youths and his investigation of the origins of the skinhead subculture in the United States. This chapter is one of the few scholarly examinations of skinheads as social street gangs.

Simi, Pete, Lowell Smith, and Ann M. S. Reeser. "From Punk Kids to Public Enemy Number One." *Deviant Behavior* 29 (2008): 753–774.
This article examines the origins and development of the Southern California–based racist skinhead gang known as Public Enemy Number One (PENI), and their attempt to balance a white supremacist and street gang identity.

"Skinhead Mayhem." *Time* 132, no. 22 (November 1988): 29.
This brief article outlines the rise of many racist skinhead groups across the United States. It focuses on the death of Ethiopian immigrant Mulugeta Seraw in Portland, Oregon.

Strauss, Neil. "The Sound of New York: Ska. Ska? Yes, Ska." *New York Times* (October 27, 1995): C1.
An article about the resurgence of Ska music in the United States, specifically the New York Ska scene. The article traces the music's popularity in the dance clubs and the prominent bands and record labels.

Suall, Irwin, David Lowe, and Michael Lieberman. *Shaved for Battle: Skinheads Target America's Youth*. ADL Special Report. New York: Anti-Defamation League of B'nai B'rith/Civil Rights Division, 1987.
One of the first publications to track the spread of skinheads in the United States. This report is full of examples of crimes and skinhead gangs across the United States. While it primarily focuses on the white supremacist groups, there is mention of antiracist skinhead groups and the fighting between the two groups.

Van Biema, David, and Massimo Calabresi. "When White Makes Right." *Time* 142 (August 1993): 40.
A prime example of the news stories that ran about skinheads between the late 1980s and early 1990s. *Time* magazine looks at the White Student Union (WSU) and other examples of white supremacists.

Watson, Gavin. *Skins*. London: Independent Music, 2001.
A collection of skinhead pictures from the late 1970s and early 1980s. Gavin Watson originally took these images of his friends and later compiled them into a photo book. He has also published other books related to the punk and skinhead subculture.

Wood, Robert. "The Indigenous, Nonracist Origins of the American Skinhead Subculture." *Youth and Society* 31 (1999): 131–151.
  The only research study about the American skinhead subculture that examines the roots of the New York hardcore scene as one of the major influences on the youth cult.

Wooden, Wayne S., and Randy Blazak. "Skinheads: Teenagers and Hate Crimes." In Wayne S. Wooden and Randy Blazak, eds. *Renegade Kids, Suburban Outlaw: From Youth Culture to Delinquency.* 2nd ed. Belmont, CA: Wadsworth, 1995: 129–154.
  This chapter is an examination of both racist and nonracist skinheads in Southern California. It provides a history of the subculture as well as interviews with 32 skinheads regarding their views and affiliation with the subculture.

Essential Electronic Sources

"A Skinhead's Secret." *Intelligence Report* 122 (Summer 2006). http://www.splcenter .org, accessed January 2, 2012.
  An interview with Jon Daly about why he became affiliated with the racist skinhead organization the American Front even though he was raised in the Jewish faith.

Anti-Racist Action. "Anti-Racist Action Home Page." Last updated December 9, 2011. http://antiracistaction.org/, accessed January 2, 2012.
  The official website for the still active chapters of ARA. Now not just a skinhead organization, ARA continues actively fighting and protesting racist groups across the United States; chapters in Europe are also active. This site reports the events of the group and stories related to fighting racism.

Blood and Honour International. "Blood and Honour Home Page." Last updated February 2011. http://www.bloodandhonour.org, accessed January 2, 2012.
  This racist website provides information on the history of the organization, links to chapters, and information on white supremacist events worldwide. Blood and Honour International has continued to be the most active white supremacist skinhead organization worldwide.

FBI Hate Crimes Division. http://www.fbi.gov/about-us/investigate/civilrights/ hate_crimes accessed January 2, 2012.
  This site is a collection of all data and reports collected by the Federal Bureau of Investigation (FBI). While most of the hate crimes reported were not committed by skinheads, it is still relevant for anyone researching racist skinhead organizations. An important note in regard to these data is that hate crimes information was not collected by the FBI until 1992—much later than when the majority of skinhead-related hate crimes took place (in the late 1980s and early 1990s).

Frank 151 Chapter 33: DMS. Summer 2008. http://www.frank151.com/book/ chap33, accessed January 2, 2012.
  This entire issue of the underground *Frank 151* magazine focuses on the history of DMS, one of the most notorious skinhead gangs of New York City. It traces

the group's history from the early Lower East Side hardcore scene to the current affiliations of what has become a music-based empire. The issue includes interviews as well as early and current pictures of the DMS crew.

Guest, Alan. "Original Skinhead Heaven" http://www.skinheadheaven.org.uk/ accessed January 4, 2012.
This British site provides information on traditional skinheads with links to music, pictures, fashion and primary documents published in English newspapers.

Hammerskin Nation. http://www.hammerskins.net/, accessed January 2, 2012.
This site provides an overview of the history of the racist organization formerly called the Hammerskins, as well as links to affiliate organizations, videos, music, and forums for member discussion.

Nutter, Chris. Skinheads.net, 1998. http/:www.skinheads.net, accessed January 2, 2012.
The first large-scale skinhead based social networking site in the United States. From the home page: "This is the largest NON-Racist and NON-Political skinhead site on the Internet. It is a Non-Political Forum where skinheads from many different countries and political backgrounds come to talk about all sorts of things."

Racist Skinhead Project. http://www.adl.org/racist_skinheads/, accessed January 2, 2012.
This website produced by the Anti-Defamation League is dedicated to tracking the activities of racist skinheads and other related groups. It includes an interactive map and recent news related to white supremacists.

Snyder, Matt. "Skinheads at Forty: Twenty Years after Their Heyday, the Antiracist Baldies Recount the Rise and Fall of a Notorious Twin Cities Scene." *City Pages* (Minneapolis/St. Paul, Minnesota) (February 20, 2008). http://www.citypages.com/2008-02-20/feature/skinheads-at-forty/.
An interview with the founding members of the anti-racist group called the Baldies 20 years after the skinhead scene started in Minneapolis.

Subcultz. http://www.subcultz.com/blog/ accessed January 4, 2012.
This site is a collection of articles related to skinheads and punk subcultures worldwide. This site will provide information not just on the United States and England but skinhead scenes in Asia and South America as well.

Wyman, Bill. "Skinheads." *Chicago Reader* (March 23, 1989). http//www.chicagoreader.com/, accessed November 10, 2010.
A feature story on the early days of the skinhead scene in Chicago, Illinois, this article details the exploits of local skinheads. Many of the individuals featured in the story were the first skinheads in the city and helped shape the concept of skinhead for youths across the United States regardless of their political affiliation.

Index

About the Authors

TIFFINI A. TRAVIS received her Master's in Library and Information Science from the University of California at Los Angeles. She is librarian and liaison for the Communication Studies Department at California State University, Long Beach. She specializes in research for popular culture, communication theory and rhetoric. She has authored numerous publications in the field of information science.

PERRY HARDY is a bass player for the Templars, a skinhead band. His travels with the band take him all over the United States, as well as to Germany and the United Kingdom. He has been active in the skinhead scene since the mid-1980s and published the popular fanzine *Carry No Banners* from 1990 until 1992. The publication was distributed throughout the United States, Europe, and Japan.